# THE PHILOSOPHY OF NOT GIVING A DAMN

## A GUIDE TO EMOTIONAL FREEDOM AND INNER STRENGTH

## THESTELLARNOMAD

*To the quiet rebels, the overthinkers, the ones who felt too much in a world that never paused.
This is for you.
For every time you swallowed your voice, held back your truth, or broke under the weight of expectations—
May these pages remind you:
You don't have to care about everything.
Just enough to stay free.*

# Contents

# Foreword

*I didn't write this book because I mastered the art of not caring.*
*I wrote it because I was drowning in caring too much.*

*Every look, every comment, every silence—I took it personally.*
*I obsessed over how I looked, how I spoke, whether I fit in, whether I was "enough."*
*Until I realized something simple, almost stupid:*
*Most of it didn't matter.*
*And the stuff that did? I'd buried under layers of fake smiles and forced politeness.*

*This book is not about becoming heartless.*
*It's about becoming selective.*
*About choosing where your energy goes, what gets your attention, and what doesn't deserve a second thought.*
*It's about reclaiming your power in a world that profits from your insecurity.*

*I'm 16. I've been called dramatic, emotional, overthinking, intense—*
*And maybe I am.*
*But this is my rebellion.*
*A quiet, inner revolution where I choose to care on my terms.*
*Where I stop chasing perfection, stop trying to fix*

*everyone, and start focusing on the only project that really matters—*
*Myself.*


*If you're reading this, maybe you're tired too.*
*Tired of being too available, too afraid, too "nice."*
*This book won't give you all the answers.*
*But it will help you ask the right questions.*


*Let's begin.*

— [the stellar nomad]

# Preface

*I didn't grow up planning to write a book.*
*But I grew up feeling everything way too deeply—and*
*eventually, I had to do something with all that weight.*

*The Art of Not Caring was born from breakdowns,*
*silent overthinking, awkward silences, sleepless*
*nights, and the kind of emotional exhaustion that*
*makes you question your whole existence.*
*And yet, what started as pain turned into something*
*else—perspective.*

*This isn't a book about being cold or heartless.*
*It's about building emotional muscle.*
*It's about walking through fire and coming out lighter,*
*not burned.*

*I wrote this as a conversation I wish someone had*
*with me years ago.*
*One that told me it's okay to say "no," to not chase*
*approval, to stop explaining yourself to people who*
*will never understand you.*
*One that reminded me: you are not your likes, your*
*followers, your past mistakes, or anyone's opinion.*

*If even one chapter helps you breathe a little easier, think a little clearer, or walk a little freer, then this book has done its job.*

x

*This is for the version of me that almost gave up—*
*And for the version of you that's still holding on.*

*Keep going.*
*And more importantly...*
*Start letting go.*

— [the stellar nomad]

# Acknowledgements

*To the people who hurt me, doubted me, left me, misunderstood me—*
*thank you.*
*You gave me the pain I needed to wake up, to grow, to write this.*


*To every moment I felt alone, confused, or invisible—*
*you taught me that silence can be a teacher too.*
*And from that silence, I found my voice.*


*To my younger self:*
*You didn't know how strong you were.*
*But I promise, everything you went through built the pages of this book.*


*To the few who stayed—really stayed—*
*thank you for seeing me when I didn't even see myself.*


*And to the reader:*
*Thank you for picking up these pages.*
*Thank you for caring about a book*
*that's trying to teach you how not to care so much.*
*You are not alone in your overthinking, in your tired heart, in your quiet battles.*


*This book is yours now.*

*Carry it like a mirror, or a weapon, or a whisper—whatever you need.*

— [the stellar nomad]

# Prologue

*There comes a moment—quiet, unnoticed—*
*when something inside you breaks.*
*Not loudly. Not violently.*
*Just... a shift.*
*Like a string snapping inside your chest.*
*And suddenly, you're tired.*

*Tired of explaining yourself.*
*Tired of being polite when you're burning inside.*
*Tired of shrinking to fit into rooms you were never*
*meant for.*

*That moment, as painful as it is,*
*is also the beginning of something else—*
*a strange kind of freedom.*

*Because once you stop caring about what doesn't*
*matter,*
*you start focusing on what does.*
*You stop playing roles.*
*You stop over-apologizing.*
*You stop chasing validation like it's oxygen.*

*This book isn't about turning off your emotions.*
*It's about turning off the noise.*
*It's about learning to protect your energy,*
*to set fire to the expectations that suffocate you,*

*and to walk through this world as your true self,*
*not the edited version they want.*


*If you've ever felt like you're too much,*
*or not enough,*
*or both at once—*
*this is your story too.*


*Let's begin where most people stop.*
*At the moment you finally say:*
*"I don't care anymore."*


*And mean it.*

— [the stellar nomad]

## CHAPTER ONE

# WHY YOU DON'T HAVE TO CARE

*Hey, my name is Mayank, better known as "The Staller nomad" Since childhood, I've been a happy kid who does whatever he wants. But as time passed, I realized that people's behavior wasn't always the same. I started thinking, What am I doing wrong? because I'm a simple boy who says the truth without thinking too much and just does what he wants.*

*When I turned 13, I started feeling different from kids my age. They acted like someone was always watching them, like there was an invisible camera on them. It seemed as though they had to avoid doing certain things on their own, without their parents' approval. For example, they didn't want to wear sandals because they feared people would laugh at them. They didn't want to hang out with all their friends because they were worried a girl might be watching. But I ignored these concerns and continued to live the way I wanted.*

*Then, when I turned 14, things started to change even more. My family members began telling me to behave the way others expected me to. I didn't understand it back then. One day, I went to the mall with my brother and cousin to watch a movie. After the movie, we were walking around, and I ran a little and did a two-step circular dance move—just something spontaneous, like anyone might do.*

*But then, I overheard my brothers talking. They said that they would like to do things like that too, but it doesn't look good if people see you doing it. That's when I really started thinking about how much people care about what others think, rather than being true to themselves.*

*Some people believe that we should care about others' views, but the point of this book is simple: we don't have to care.*

## The Influence of Judgment

*Nowadays, people care about every little thing when it comes to how others judge them. They become so concerned with what others think that they forget how to be themselves. Here are some examples of things people care about without even realizing it:*

- 

*Accent or way of speaking*

- *Financial status*

- *Tattoos or piercings*

- *Hobbies or interests*

- *Academic qualifications*

- *Popularity in social groups*

- *House size or decor*

- *Political views*

- *How they spend their free time*

- *Pets or types of animals owned*

*The point here isn't that you can't get a tattoo, buy a pet, or pursue academics—you can do whatever you want. The problem arises when people do these things just to fit in. For example, getting a tattoo because it's "cool," buying a pet because everyone else has one, or pursuing academics just because it's what everyone else is doing. That's wrong. You shouldn't care about what others are doing; the key is to focus on whether you truly want to do it.*

*That's where the art of not caring comes in.*

## Why We Don't Have to Care

*As we go through life, there are people who will try to make us fit into their mold, judge us, or tell us what we should and shouldn't do. But the truth is, we don't need to care about what others think. In fact, embracing who we truly are — regardless of judgment — is often the key to success and happiness.*

*Here are some real-life stories of people who didn't let society's judgment hold them back and ended up making a significant impact on the world:*

### Steve Jobs

*Steve Jobs, co-founder of Apple, is one of the most well-known figures who ignored societal judgment. He was often criticized for his unorthodox thinking and demanding management style. People doubted his ideas, but he stayed true to his vision. Jobs wasn't concerned with what others thought; his focus was on* innovation and creating products that would change the world. His perseverance led to the creation of Apple, a company that revolutionized technology and became a global powerhouse. Jobs showed us that when you trust your vision and don't care about being judged, you can achieve great things.

## Oprah Winfrey

Oprah Winfrey's story is another powerful example. She came from a background of poverty and faced many challenges, including harsh judgment from people who doubted her ability to succeed in television. She was told that she wasn't fit for the media industry and that her style of interviewing wouldn't work. Despite the negativity, Oprah remained authentic and continued to follow her passion. Today, she is one of the most influential media figures in the world. Her journey reminds us that by not caring about the judgment of others, we can build our own path to success.

## Lady Gaga

Lady Gaga is a pop icon who built her career by being unapologetically herself. In the early stages of her career, people criticized her for her unique fashion sense and bold, artistic expression. They said she would never make it because she didn't fit the traditional pop star mold. But Lady Gaga didn't care. She embraced her individuality, and in doing so, she *became a global superstar. Her message to the world, especially through songs like "Born This Way," is clear: don't care about judgment and love yourself for who you are.*

## Richard Branson

*Richard Branson, founder of the Virgin Group, is another great example of someone who didn't let people's opinions define him. He took risks, followed his dreams, and didn't care if people doubted him. From starting Virgin Records with no experience to trying extreme sports and breaking world records, Branson's success came from being true to himself and not worrying about others' judgments. His life proves that when you stay focused on your goals and ignore negativity, anything is possible.*

## Ellen DeGeneres

*Ellen DeGeneres, known for her humor and kindness, faced significant backlash when she publicly came out as gay in 1997. Her sitcom was canceled shortly after, and many thought her career was over. However, Ellen didn't let the judgment affect her. She stayed true to who she was, and years later, became one of the most beloved talk show hosts in America. Ellen's story teaches us that embracing who you are, even in the face of criticism, can lead to unexpected success and fulfillment.*

## Conclusion

*These are just a few examples of people who didn't care about the judgment of others. Instead of allowing negativity and societal pressure to define them, they stayed true to their passions and their authentic selves. And look where it got them! They became pioneers in their fields and icons for others to follow.*

*The key takeaway is this: We don't have to care about others' judgments. Success and happiness come from living authentically and following our own paths, not from trying to meet others' expectations. So, let go of the fear of judgment and embrace your true self — because, in the end, that's what truly matters.*

## Live Your Life

*I didn't tell you these stories to motivate you or anything. They are meant to show you the mirror of reality — to reflect how life truly is. So, forget about the embarrassment, the judgment, or any obstacles in your way, and just do what you want. It's your life, and you're the one in control.*

*Follow your own path, not someone else's. You are not the main character in everyone else's story; you are the main character in your own story.*

*Chase your dreams.*

## *Chapter Summary: Why We Don't Have to Care*

1.

### *Introduction to Journey*
*Mayank, known as "The Staller," grew up as a free-spirited individual who did whatever he wanted without worrying about others' opinions.*

2.

### *Adapting to Social Expectations*
*At age 13, Mayank noticed a shift in behavior among his peers, who were increasingly concerned with how others saw them. This led to a realization that people often live based on others' judgments, instead of being true to themselves.*

3.

### *The Influence of Judgment*
*People today care about judgments in every aspect of life— from appearance and interests to lifestyle choices like tattoos, pets, and political views. However, this focus on fitting in often detracts from individual authenticity.*

4.

### The Art of Not Caring
*The key takeaway is simple: we shouldn't care about others' views. Success and happiness come from staying true to ourselves, not from following what others think is right for us.*

5.

### Real-Life Examples of Not Caring
*The stories of icons like Steve Jobs, Oprah Winfrey, Lady Gaga, Richard Branson, and Ellen DeGeneres serve as powerful reminders of how ignoring societal judgment can lead to success and personal fulfillment.*

6.

### Embracing Your True Self
*These individuals faced harsh criticism and judgment but stayed authentic to their vision. Their success was a result of focusing on their dreams, not on fitting into society's mold.*

7.

### Don't Let Judgment Define You
*The message is clear: don't let judgment shape who you are. Live your life authentically, chase your dreams, and follow your own path—because in the end, you are the main character in your own story.*

8.

### Live Your Life
*Forget the fear of judgment and embrace who you truly are. Life is too short to live according to others' expectations. It's your life, so make it count.*

## CHAPTER TWO

# THE CRINGE TRAP

## Hiding Behind the Word "Cringe"

*I've got something to say, and it's not going to sound too nice: today's generation has a word they hide behind—"**cringe.**" It's a word that gets thrown around whenever something feels uncomfortable or out of place. It's harsh, I know, but hear me out: some people want something but never do it—or they can't. So, they label it as "cringe." But why? What's the reason behind that? For me, when we want something but society's judgment holds us back, that's when it becomes "cringe."*

*I remember a time when a friend and I went to a popular tourist spot in India. We hadn't seen each other in a while, and I was looking forward to catching up. He's a bit older than me and now has a steady job, so he came straight from his 9-to-5 in his formal clothes. When I saw him, he looked so different. It wasn't that he was more serious than before—we've always talked about deep stuff together. But there was something else. He looked like someone who had just been strapped to a chair, unable to move. It wasn't like he had changed, but there was this weight to him, almost like he was carrying a heavy burden. I thought to myself, Maybe it's just what happens when you grow up.*

*As we were talking, the rain suddenly started pouring down. We rushed to stand under a tree, and that's when I noticed a group of college students, probably from out of state, enjoying the rain. Out of nowhere, they started dancing. And it wasn't the kind of dancing that was concerned with looking silly or getting wet—it was free. They were dancing like they had nothing to lose, like they were completely in the moment.*

*When my friend saw them, he immediately called them "cringe." But as he said it, I couldn't help but notice how his words didn't match the way he was looking at them. He was staring at them with this sort of longing. The way he reached out his hand to feel the rain, the way his eyes followed the dancing... it was almost like he wanted to join in. He wanted to let go, to stop caring about what people thought. But something was holding him back—his formal clothes, the adult responsibilities he'd taken on, and the judgment of society.*

*I know this isn't a textbook example of "cringe," but it stuck with me. We all hide behind that word at some point, don't we? We use it to dismiss things we're too afraid to try or understand. We call something "cringe" because it's easier than admitting that it makes us uncomfortable, or that we wish we could be like that too.*

*But here's the thing: sometimes, "cringe" isn't about something being awkward or embarrassing. It's about society telling us how we should act, what we should wear, and how we should behave. And sometimes, it's about us holding ourselves back, afraid to let go of that need for approval.*

*That moment with my friend taught me something. We don't have to hide behind the word "cringe" to explain why we don't step outside our comfort zone. Maybe, instead of labeling things as "cringe," we should ask ourselves what's really stopping us from just being free, like those in the rain.*

*I have some stories as well to explain this better*

## 1. The Awkward Friend

*Jenna was scrolling through her phone when Amy, her best friend, showed her a video of a dance trend she'd just learned. Amy's eyes sparkled as she played it, waiting for Jenna's reaction. Jenna stared at the screen for a moment, unsure how to respond.*

*"Ugh, that's so cringe," Jenna said, laughing awkwardly.*

*Amy's smile dropped, just for a second, but Jenna didn't see it. She quickly backtracked, "I mean, it's just... not really my thing, you know?"*

*But inside, Jenna felt terrible. She hated how judgmental she sounded. If she were being honest, she admired Amy's confidence—Jenna could never do something like that. But she couldn't let Amy see that. So, she pretended like she didn't care, even though a small part of her wanted to try the dance too.*

## 2. The Overconfident Comment

*After the movie, the group of friends was chatting about it, when Mark started talking about this indie band he'd been really into. "They're kinda cool," he said, "but some of their songs are low-key cringe."*

*Ethan snorted, trying to act like he agreed. "Yeah, I can't deal with how cheesy their lyrics are. It's just too much."*

*But in reality, Ethan had been obsessed with one of their songs for the past week. It had been stuck in his head non-stop. He just didn't want to admit it to the group. If he did, they'd probably make fun of him for liking something "weird." So, he kept it cool, pretending he was totally unaffected, even though his heart gave a little squeeze of regret.*

## 3. The Unspoken Apology

*Mia and Lucy had been friends forever. When Mia showed up in a new outfit she was really excited about, Lucy didn't hold back. "Wow, that's... kind of cringe. You look like you're trying way too hard."*

*Mia froze. Her heart sank, and for a second, she wondered if she'd made a mistake. Lucy seemed to notice the shift in her friend's face, and quickly added, "I didn't mean it like that. I'm sorry. I just don't really get the vibe, that's all."*

*Mia smiled weakly, not wanting to make things awkward, but she couldn't help feeling hurt. Later that day, Mia put the outfit on again, standing in front of the mirror, trying to convince herself it wasn't a big deal. But deep down, she wished Lucy hadn't said it. Instead of confronting her, Mia just kept quiet, pretending she wasn't bothered when, in truth, she really was.*

**Understanding the Word "Cringe"**

*The concept of "cringe" is one we all know, but have you ever stopped to consider why it exists in the first place? How did this word come into being, and what does it really mean for those who use it? In my opinion, the term "cringe" was created by people who simply don't enjoy life.*

*Think about it. Who doesn't dream of hopping into a car, driving up to the mountains, and leaving behind the weight of the world? Who wouldn't want the confidence to grab a camera, vlog in public like a seasoned influencer, or sing and dance without fear in front of a crowd? Yet, so many people hold back. Why? Because they fear judgment or embarrassment. And when faced with this hesitation, what do we do? We dismiss it, acting as though we don't care.*

*But here's where things get interesting. That dismissal, that indifference we show, is precisely the thing we care about most. The truth is, you don't have to care about other people's opinions on what you care about. And understanding this is key to freeing yourself from unnecessary worries.*

*Some people misinterpret the "art of not caring" to mean they shouldn't care about anything. But that's not the point. The real lesson is this: You must care about the things that matter to you—your dreams, your passions, the things that make you who you are. Because at the end of the day, these things belong to you. They aren't dictated by some random person's judgment. You don't need to concern yourself with how their mind works, or how they perceive you. The only thing that will bring you true happiness is being yourself. And that, in the end, is what will always matter.*

*Some might argue that what they do is far too significant for others to ignore, that everyone around them is constantly watching their every move. In reality, however, people often overestimate just how much others actually care about them. The truth is, most people are so wrapped up in their own lives that they hardly notice what others are doing. To help understand why this happens, I decided to explore some psychological concepts that explain why we tend to think others care more than they really do.*

## *Why We Think People Care More Than They Actually Do*

*There are moments in life when we feel like the entire world is staring at us, judging every word we say, every step we take. Maybe it's because of an outfit we're unsure about, or perhaps a social mistake that we think will haunt us. In those moments, it can feel like the spotlight is shining directly on us. But the truth is, most of the time, people are not paying as much attention to us as we think.*

### *The Spotlight Effect*
*This phenomenon is known as the spotlight effect—the belief that we are the center of attention.*

*In reality, people are far more focused on their own lives, their own problems, than we realize. We often assume that others are constantly observing us, but in fact, they are probably caught up in their own world, just as we are with ours.*

### Social Comparison Theory

*Another reason we often feel as if people are watching us comes from social comparison theory. As humans, we tend to measure ourselves against others. This leads us to believe that our actions, our behavior, and even our appearance are being scrutinized by everyone around us. But the reality is that most people are too busy with their own lives to notice the small details we worry about. They are not thinking about us nearly as much as we imagine.*

### Egocentrism

*Humans are naturally egocentric—we see the world through the lens of our own experiences and concerns. It's easy to assume that everyone else is noticing the same things we obsess over. But the truth is, most people are so caught up in their own lives that they rarely give much thought to what others are doing.*

### Gilovich's Experiment

*In an experiment conducted by psychologist Thomas Gilovich, participants wore an embarrassing t-shirt in public, believing that everyone would notice it and judge them. But when researchers asked people what they had noticed, most people hadn't even seen the shirt! This experiment reveals how overestimating* *attention can lead us to feel more self-conscious than we need to be. (Thomas Gilovich's experiment was conducted in **the late 1990s**. The exact year of the experiment isn't always specified, but it was part of his broader research into self-consciousness and social psychology, particularly the spotlight effect, which he and his colleagues began exploring in the mid-90s)*

*In Thomas Gilovich's experiment, people were asked to wear an embarrassing t-shirt in public, expecting that everyone would notice and judge them. It's a scenario we've all likely imagined in some form—thinking that a mistake, a weird outfit, or something else we're self-conscious about is obvious to everyone around us. We're convinced that the spotlight is on us, making every tiny flaw feel huge.*

*But here's the twist: when researchers later asked people what they had noticed about the person in the t-shirt, the majority hadn't even seen it. This experiment highlights something important—we tend to believe everyone is paying attention to our every move when, in reality, people are usually too focused on themselves to even notice.*

*The experiment is a clear example of the spotlight effect—that feeling we get that everyone is staring at us, judging us, or picking apart everything we do. But the truth is, people are rarely as concerned with us as we think. They're wrapped up in their own world, their own worries, and they don't have the time or energy to scrutinize us as much as we imagine.*

*What Gilovich's experiment really shows us is that the things we worry so much about—our mistakes, our awkward moments, our insecurities—are often invisible to the people around us. And even if they do notice, it's not a big deal. People are generally not as focused on us as we fear. This can be a huge relief because it means we don't need to stress about being judged nearly as much as we think we do. Instead of overthinking what others might think, we can just be ourselves and let go of that unnecessary pressure.*

## Chapter Ending

*In the end of this chapter, I want to leave you with one thing: don't let anyone else—good or bad—define your worth. Be positive in the way you look at things. If you want to dance in the rain, then go dance in the rain. If you want to make a funny video, make it. If you want to start singing, release your song. If you want to travel the world, pack your bags and go. Don't wait for others to show you the way.*

*Don't be a copy—be yourself. Because the world doesn't care about you as much as you think. So why should you care what others think? <u>Remember, the people who call others "cringe" are often the ones who don't know how to be happy in their own lives</u>. So, be yourself.*

*If you want to do something, just do it*


**Chapter Summary : The Cringe Trap**


· **The Word "Cringe"**: *The chapter discusses how the word "cringe" is often used to dismiss things we're too afraid to try or understand, especially when societal judgment holds us back.*


· **The Friend's Transformation**: *The author reflects on a moment when a friend, who seemed weighed down by adult responsibilities, called a group of dancing college students "cringe" while secretly longing to join them, revealing the tension between wanting freedom and fearing judgment.*


· **Using "Cringe" to Avoid Vulnerability**: *The author points out that labeling things as "cringe" is often a defense mechanism to avoid confronting our own discomfort or insecurities.*


· **Challenging Societal Expectations**: *The chapter emphasizes that "cringe" is often about society's narrow expectations of behavior, clothing, and expression, and how these pressures limit our freedom.*

· ***Being Yourself****: The main message is that we should stop worrying about how others perceive us. Instead, we should focus on doing what truly matters to us—whether it's pursuing passions or expressing ourselves freely.*

· ***Psychological Insights****: The chapter explores the psychological reasons why we overestimate the attention others pay to us, referencing concepts like the Spotlight Effect, Social Comparison Theory, and Egocentrism.*

· ***Gilovich's Experiment****: Psychologist Thomas Gilovich's experiment demonstrates how we tend to overestimate how much others notice our perceived flaws, suggesting that we're not as under scrutiny as we think.*

· ***Final Thought****: The chapter ends with the idea that we should let go of fear and judgment, encouraging readers to follow their dreams and be true to themselves without worrying about societal labels or expectations.*

## CHAPTER THREE

# THE ONE DAY THEORY

## Mastering the Art of Not Caring

*Now, I'm sure everyone understands the concept I'm presenting, but some of you may be wondering: we care so much about things, so how do we stop? How do we master the art of not caring? The truth is, it's simpler than you might think. First, let me share a few essential points on how to let go of things that don't truly matter and focus only on what does. Once you begin to apply these ideas, it becomes much easier to stop letting everything overwhelm you.*

## Key Principles for Letting Go:

•

*Prioritize What Matters: Focus on the things that truly impact your life. If something doesn't add value, let it go.*

- *Control What You Can: Acknowledge that you can't control everything, and that's perfectly okay. Focus on what you can change and accept the rest.*

- *Stop Seeking Approval: Stop worrying about what others think. If you're content with yourself, that's all that truly matters.*

- *Practice Detachment: Get comfortable with letting go of attachments to specific outcomes, people, or objects. It will free you from unnecessary stress.*

- *Embrace Imperfection: Life is inherently messy. You can't have everything perfect all the time. Sometimes, accepting imperfections is the key to letting go.*

- *Don't Overthink: The more you think, the more you care. Try to take things at face value, and avoid overanalyzing every detail.*

- *Set Boundaries: Protect your energy. If something or someone drains you, it's okay to say no and step away.*

- **Mindfulness:** *Be present in the moment. Worrying about the past or future only adds unnecessary stress.*

*With these principles in mind, we can now dive deeper into how much you care and how that directly affects the growth of your hope. Let me illustrate this with a story:*

## The Weight of Hope

*There was a guy named Leo who always cared. He cared about everything—the way people felt, their struggles, and their victories. He put his heart into his friendships, always checking in on others, making sure they were okay. He believed that if he was kind enough, people would see him, appreciate him, and treat him with the same care he gave.*

*For a while, it seemed to work. He got smiles, thanks, and occasional moments of connection that made him think maybe his kindness was being returned. His hope grew stronger. He thought, "If I just keep being this way, the world will treat me the same." He gave pieces of himself, thinking it would eventually come back to him.*

*But over time, things started to change. The smiles faded, the kind gestures stopped, and Leo began to notice that people weren't as present when he needed them. He'd been there for others in their hardest moments, but when it was his turn to lean on someone, he felt alone. His friends didn't seem to notice his pain, his struggles. It wasn't that they were bad people—it was just that they didn't seem to care in the way he hoped.*

*Leo felt his heart sink. He gave so much of himself, but nobody seemed to care as much. The world he thought would reflect his kindness didn't. The more he hoped, the emptier he felt. The weight of unreturned care started to break him down.*

*He thought if he kept trying, kept being the person who cared for everyone else, it would pay off. But it didn't. The disappointment piled up, and soon, the hope he once had seemed like a distant memory. He couldn't keep giving when no one seemed to notice or care about him.*

*One day, Leo realized something important: the world might not treat him the way he treated others, but he had to learn to take care of himself. He couldn't keep pouring from an empty cup. Even though it hurt, he understood that the kindness he gave didn't always come back from the people he expected. But that didn't mean he had to stop being who he was. He just had to find the strength to care for himself and let go of the hope that things would always balance out the way he wanted.*

## *Living Life Like It's Your Last Day*

*Yeah, I know everyone has felt lost in life at some point. I was there too. But what truly matters is how you learn from life's lessons—whether through experience or the wisdom you gain from books. The thing is simple: just open your eyes and see the truth.*

*I remember a long time ago when I first heard a quote, and it really gave me goosebumps. The quote goes like this:*

**"Some wake up at 50.**
**Some wake up at 30.**
**Some wake up at 18.**
**And some never wake up. It's your choice."**

*It's an amazing quote if you understand its meaning. Now, I'm about to give you the best tip to learn the art of not caring. It's something I personally tried, and let me tell you, it was amazing. What I'm talking about here is something I've named: **One Day of Being Yourself.***

*It's an amazing practice. First, I'm going to give you some details, then I'll show you how I put it into practice.*

## ONE DAY OF BEING YOURSELF

*Some time ago, I was trapped in this social cycle, just like you. I felt messed up, and I couldn't decide what to do. But then, I made one decision. It's also a theory of mine, and it goes like this:* **A single day can change anything in your life.**

*And you just have to find that one day. So, how do you find it? It's about anything, but right now in this book, we're talking about the art of not caring. We'll focus on that, but this theory can be applied to anything in your life.*

*I can't say more right now because this is my personal theory, but who knows? I might write a whole book on it someday. For now, let's focus on how to use* **one day of being yourself** *to learn the art of not caring. It's practical, and you have to do it.*

*The deal is simple: for just one day, be the person you want to be. Don't be a crybaby, don't make excuses, and just do it. Here's the plan. Follow these points for one day and see what happens.*

### *Live for One Day Like You Want:*

1.

**Let Go of Judgment** *Stop worrying about what others think of you. Whether it's how you dress, talk, or act, the only opinion that matters is yours. Be authentic and embrace who you are.*

2.

**Do What Feels Right** *If you've always wanted to do something, whether big or small, take the leap today. Dance in public, sing out loud, take an impromptu trip, or try that hobby you've been thinking about. Life's too short to wait for the "perfect moment."*

3.

**Be Present** *Focus entirely on the present moment. Stop thinking about the past or future. Engage fully with what you're doing—whether it's talking to someone, watching the sunset, or simply being alone with your thoughts.*

4.

**Break Free from Routine** *Shake up your usual habits. Maybe go off the beaten path, change your routine, or leave your comfort zone. Do something spontaneous that excites you, without overthinking it.*

5.

**Follow Your Own Path** *Don't let the expectations of others hold you back. You have your own dreams, goals, and desires. Pursue what feels right for you,* *even if it's different from what others expect.*

6.

**Do What Makes You Happy** *What brings you pure joy? Find it, embrace it, and let it be your focus for the day. Whether it's spending time with loved ones, being alone in nature, eating your favorite meal, or something else—do it!*

7.

**Laugh Like No One's Watching** *Find humor in the small things, and let go of any inhibitions. Don't be afraid to laugh loud, even if it's at yourself. Life is too short to take seriously all the time.*

8.

**Be Kind, but Don't Overthink It** *Help others or spread positivity if it feels right, but don't feel obligated. Just do it because it aligns with your inner peace, not because you have to.*

9.

**Take Risks** *Living as if it's your last day can mean being open to the unknown. Maybe it's finally texting someone you've been avoiding or making that bold decision you've been hesitating on. Embrace risks that will make you feel alive.*

10.

**Embrace the Freedom of Imperfection** *Let go of trying to be perfect. Mistakes and mess-ups are part of life, and they make you who you are. Celebrate the imperfect, the quirky, and the real parts of yourself.*

11.

*Connect with Nature* *Spend time outdoors, breathing in fresh air, feeling the sun on your face, or watching the stars. Nature has a way of helping us reconnect with ourselves and reminds us of how small and beautiful life can be.*

12.

*Live With Gratitude* *Gratitude brings focus to the present and shifts your mindset. Appreciate the small things—your health, a good conversation, the beauty around you. It grounds you in the here and now.*

13.

*Forgive and Let Go* *Don't carry old grudges or regrets with you. Life's too short to hold onto negativity. If there's something or someone you need to forgive, do it today. Let go of anything weighing you down emotionally.*

14.

*Express Love Freely* *Tell the people you care about how much they mean to you, without reservation. Show love in any form—whether it's through words, actions, or gestures. Don't wait for a "special occasion."*

15.

*Embrace Silence and Solitude* *If you're someone who's always busy or surrounded by people, take a moment to be alone with your thoughts. Embrace the peace that comes with solitude. Sometimes, the best way to live fully is to just be.*

*Because no one is watching you for just one day, wear that weird dress that people say isn't "good" but that you like. Wear that strange hat, or eat your favorite food. Go to your favorite place, play the music, or dance like a kid. At the end of the day, what you did will feel good to you.*

*The happiness you're searching for isn't somewhere else. It's within you. You are the key to that happiness. And when you get it, you'll realize what truly makes you feel happy.*

*Maybe, after that day, you'll start following your passion. But even if you don't, you'll have learned one important thing: **The only thing that matters is you. No one else.** And yeah, this isn't just some lame theory. I've personally tried it, and it changed my life.*

*Now, let me show you how I spent that day.*

### *That One Day of My Life: The Day I Decided to Be Me*

*It didn't start with fireworks. No big drama. Just a feeling deep inside me that said, "Enough." Enough of trying to fit in, enough of hiding the parts of me that felt too weird, too much, too different for the world. I was done being careful. That day, I gave myself full permission to be who I really was—no filters, no apologies.*

*I threw on this white anime T-shirt I loved. Not "stylish," not "normal," but something that felt like me. Usually I'd overthink it. I'd be like, "Nah, people will judge." But not that day. That day, I looked in the mirror and thought, "This is me. Let them stare."*

*I went straight to a music studio. No plan. I just walked in, sat down, and started messing with sounds. I played a few chords on the guitar, adjusted some knobs, let the rhythm carry me. I wasn't making a hit song or trying to impress anyone. I was just vibing, letting the music speak a language only I needed to understand.*

*Then I hit a library. Another place people wouldn't expect. The silence felt sacred. I picked up a random book, sat down, and just read—something I hadn't done in a while without distractions. It was just me, the pages, and peace.*

*Later, I played guitar again—this time alone, no mic, no audience. Just me and the strings, talking in a way words never could. It felt like coming home to a part of myself I'd been neglecting.*

*But the real shift happened when I decided to go to the movies—alone. That might not sound like a big deal, but for me? It was a whole statement.*

*See, I've always loved movies. They weren't just entertainment—they were escape, therapy, friends, teachers. I grew up in those fantasy worlds. I felt seen in them more than I ever did by the people around me. But every time I'd ask someone to come with me, they'd judge me. "You watch too many movies." "You live in a fantasy world." They didn't get it. They never did.*

*And honestly? I got tired of asking. I got tired of defending something that's such a deep part of who I am.*

*So now, when a new fiction film comes out and I want to see it, I don't wait around anymore. I don't beg people to come. I just go. Alone. Proudly. That day, I walked into that theater, bought my ticket, grabbed my popcorn, and sat down with zero shame. I didn't feel lonely. I felt complete. Because I was doing what I love, for me.*

*No compromises. No fake conversations. No pretending to be chill about something I'm deeply passionate about.*

*And that's what this whole "One Day" is about. It's not just about doing random things. It's about remembering who you are, and finally honoring it. It's about breaking free from expectations, from judgment, from all the invisible rules we trap ourselves in.*

*That day didn't "fix" me. But it freed me. It reminded me that the only approval I really need is my own. And once you taste that kind of freedom, it's hard to go back.*

*And the last thing is "<u>stop apologizing for who you are</u>"*

*"Now, let me tell you about a life-changing moment in Jim Carrey's (known as The Truman ) life how a small moment completely changed his life.*

*The One day of Jim Carrey's*

*Jim Carrey is a Canadian-American actor, comedian, and writer known for his energetic, over-the-top comedic style. Rising to fame in the 1990s with hit films like Ace Ventura: Pet Detective, The Mask, and Liar Liar, Carrey became one of Hollywood's most beloved funnymen. His ability to blend slapstick humor with deeply emotional roles was showcased in more dramatic films like The Truman Show and Eternal Sunshine of the Spotless Mind. Known for his wild facial expressions and distinctive voice work, Carrey continues to be a versatile figure in entertainment.*

## A Wake-Up Call: The False Missile Alert in Hawaii

***January 13, 2018*** *– It was just another ordinary day for Jim Carrey in Hawaii, or so he thought. Little did he know, the world around him was about to come to a terrifying halt. On this day, Hawaii was hit with a false missile alert that warned of an inbound ballistic missile. The alarm read: "Ballistic missile threat inbound to Hawaii. Seek immediate shelter. This is not a drill."*

*For 38 minutes, residents scrambled to find shelter, say their goodbyes, and brace for what seemed like impending doom. What no one knew at the time was that the alert was a mistake—a glitch in the system—but for those 38 minutes, the fear was real.*

*Jim Carrey, living on the islands at the time, was not immune to the panic. As the sirens blared and the alert flashed on his phone, he was thrust into a moment of intense fear and uncertainty. As the minutes passed, Carrey thought to himself, "This could be it. This could be the end."*

*It was in this moment, with only about 10 minutes left before the missile was predicted to strike, that Carrey experienced a profound shift in his thinking. Instead of spiraling into panic, as most would in such a dire situation, something unexpected happened—he found himself at peace.*

*"What if I really had just 10 minutes left to live?" he thought. "Is there anything I regret? Would I be at peace with how I've lived my life?"*

*Carrey's mind wandered back to his career, his relationships, and the choices he had made. And then, in that brief moment of clarity, he realized something life-changing:* **He had lived authentically.** *In those 10 minutes, Carrey didn't feel anger, fear, or regret. He wasn't worried about the things he hadn't done or the places he hadn't been. Instead, he was grateful for the life he had lived—a life in which he had taken risks, been true to himself, and followed his passions, no matter the challenges.*

*Carrey reflected on how often people waste their time worrying about what others think of them, chasing after validation, or living according to society's expectations. But in that moment, as he considered his own mortality, he understood that none of that mattered. The only thing that mattered was whether or not he had lived a life that was true to himself.*

*As the alert came to an end, and the missile never arrived, Carrey felt a deep sense of relief—but more than that, he felt gratitude. He realized that, no matter how long he had left on this earth, the most important thing was to keep living authentically, without fear, and without regret.*

### The Life Lesson:

*The missile alert wasn't just a moment of terror—it was a profound wake-up call. For Carrey, it was a reminder that life is fragile, and none of us are guaranteed a tomorrow. But in the face of that uncertainty, he found clarity.*

*If he had truly only had 10 minutes left to live, Carrey would have died content, knowing he had lived on his own terms. That moment was a powerful reminder that, in the end, it doesn't matter how much time we have—it's about how we use it.*

*What would you do if you had 10 minutes left to live? Would you be proud of the life you've led? Would you feel fulfilled, knowing you had lived authentically? Or would you be filled with regret, wishing you had followed your passions or spoken your truth?*

*Jim Carrey's story challenges us to think about how we're living right now. Are we waiting for the "perfect moment" to start living the life we truly want? Or are we, like Carrey, already living fully, authentically, and without hesitation?*

*The lesson is clear:* **Live for yourself.** *Live in a way that, if today was your last, you could look back with no regrets, knowing that you lived true to who you are.*

**The Real Challenge:**

*Jim Carrey's experience with the false missile alert is a powerful reminder that time is fleeting. Every moment counts, and we can't afford to waste time living for anyone but ourselves. Life is fragile, and in an instant, everything can change. But in those moments of uncertainty, we can choose to be at peace with how we've lived, knowing that we've been true to our hearts.*

*So, ask yourself: How are you living right now? Are you living authentically? Are you chasing your dreams? Or are you letting fear or external pressures hold you back?*

*The truth is, the missile we're all waiting for is time itself. It's constantly moving forward, and we never know when our time will run out. But we do know that every second counts. The key is to live each moment with purpose, passion, and authenticity.*

*Because, when it all comes down to it, the real gift isn't the time we have—it's how we choose to spend*

*You can see how just one 10-minute moment in your life can change everything. And I'm talking about giving yourself just one day. I promise you, you won't regret it.*

*Now, I want to share one of the best lines from one of the greatest fictional characters of all time, from the greatest fictional show One Piece. This line shows you the best way to live your life. Every time I hear this quote, I get the instinctive feeling that no one knows when their time will come. It could be at the age of 100, 70, 40, 30, or even tomorrow. Death, after all, is the only truth. And if you run from death, you can never truly live your life properly. So, accept everything, and live an amazing life.*

*And everything I've just said comes from a single quote—because the character who says this line lives every day of his life the way he wants.*

*"I don't wanna live a thousand years. If I just live through today, that'll be enough."*
*—Portgas D. Ace*

**Live the best life, full of dreams.**

*Chase the dreams that make your heart race, the ones that set your soul on fire. Life is too short to settle for anything less than what truly excites you. Dream big, take risks, and don't be afraid to stumble along the way. Each step brings you closer to the person you're meant to be.*

**summary of chapter The one day theory**

*Dress for Yourself – Wear what makes you feel good, not what others expect.*

*Do That One Thing You've Been Postponing – Whether it's visiting a studio or going to the library, stop waiting for the "right time."*

*Enjoy Your Own Company – Go solo to places like a theater or café. Being alone doesn't mean being lonely.*

*Let Go of People-Pleasing – Make choices based on your desires, not others' opinions or judgments.*

*Capture Moments, Not for Likes – Take photos and videos for memories, not for validation on social media.*

*Ignore the Inner Critic – That voice telling you you're "cringe"? It's not real. Silence it and be free.*

*Do It All Like You're Free – Live like no one's watching—dance, sing, laugh, or cry without shame.*

*Feel the Power of Detachment – For just one day, detach from the need to fit in. It's a taste of real freedom.*

## CHAPTER FOUR

# LOVE, RELATIONSHIPS, AND THE ART OF NOT CARING

*When we talk about the art of not caring, let's get one thing straight: this isn't about cutting off people you love or treating them like they don't matter. If anything, it's the complete opposite. It's about learning how to love in a way that's free from all the pressure, the overthinking, and the unrealistic expectations we often pile on our relationships.*

*We all know that relationships can be intense. There's this constant worry, this urge to please, and, let's be honest, the fear that if we don't act a certain way or give enough, the other person might not stick around. But here's the thing: the art of not caring isn't about becoming emotionally distant or shutting people out. It's about letting go of the things that hold you back from truly connecting with someone—and, more importantly, from staying true to yourself.*

## 1. Love Doesn't Mean Possessing

*One of the biggest misconceptions people have is that love equals possession. That if you love someone, you have to own them, know everything they're doing, and control how they spend their time. But that's not love; that's control. And control isn't healthy.*

*The art of not caring means loving without clinging. It's about giving your partner the space to be themselves, to do their own thing, and trusting that they'll come back to you—not out of obligation, but because they genuinely want to. The best kind of love is the kind where both people are free to be who they are, without fear of losing each other. You can love someone deeply, but you don't need to own them to prove it.*

## 2. Let Go of the "Shoulds"

*Expectations are the silent killers of relationships. We all do it—set these huge expectations about how things should be, how our partner should act, or what they should say. But when those expectations aren't met, we get disappointed, and that disappointment builds walls between us.*

*The art of not caring is about letting go of the "shoulds." Instead of constantly worrying about how things are supposed to be, try letting the relationship unfold naturally. Give yourself and your partner permission to just be, without the pressure to live up to some perfect image of what love is supposed to look like.*

*It's not about tolerating bad behavior, but rather not expecting perfection or creating a fantasy version of someone in your mind. People are messy, and relationships are even messier—but that's where the real magic happens.*

### *3. Self-Love First, Always*

*Here's a truth many of us forget: You can't pour from an empty cup. If you're always putting your partner's needs before your own, you're setting yourself up for burnout. The art of not caring means drawing boundaries—giving yourself the time and space to recharge, to heal, to be you.*

*Loving yourself isn't selfish. It's essential. When you're in a good place emotionally, mentally, and physically, that's when you can show up fully in your relationships—not because you have to, but because you want to. You're not giving from a place of neediness or desperation; you're giving from a place of abundance.*

## 4. Say What You Mean, Mean What You Say

*We all know how games can sneak into relationships—those little "mind games" we play to see how much someone cares or how they'll react. But here's the thing: those games? They're exhausting. They create more confusion than connection. And they only serve to mask the truth.*

*Instead, the art of not caring means being straight up. If something's bothering you, say it. If you're feeling good, let your partner know. If you need space, ask for it. No passive-aggressive behavior. No pretending everything's fine when it's not. True love is built on honest communication, and that's something you don't have to carelessly tiptoe around.*

## 5. Stop Fearing Loss

*Here's the big one: the fear of losing someone. We've all been there, right? That constant worry that if we don't keep our partner happy 24/7, they'll leave. But here's the thing—love is not about fear. When love is based on fear, it's not really love at all. It's insecurity.*

*The art of not caring is about letting go of that fear. It's about realizing that love isn't about holding on tight—it's about trusting. If someone is meant to be in your life, they'll stay. If not, they won't. And that's okay. People come and go, and that doesn't mean you've failed or that you're not worthy. Sometimes, love just runs its course—and that's part of life. Learning to be okay with that is one of the most freeing things you can do for yourself.*

## 6. Family: Loving Without Losing Yourself

*When it comes to family, things can get complicated. We all love our families, but sometimes, that love comes with strings attached—expectations, pressure, guilt, and, honestly, some emotional baggage. A lot of times, we feel like we owe family everything, like we're supposed to put up with all their drama, fulfill their dreams for us, or just deal with their emotional chaos without complaining.*

*But here's the thing: loving your family doesn't mean carrying all of that. The art of not caring in family dynamics is about setting boundaries and knowing that it's okay to say, "I love you, but I can't take on your stress right now." It doesn't mean you don't care about them—it just means you're not going to let their issues or expectations define your life or steal your peace.*

*Sometimes, family can be downright toxic—whether it's constant judgment, guilt-tripping, or just overstepping boundaries. And while it might feel like you should always put family first, you don't have to sacrifice your happiness for theirs. You can still love them, but that doesn't mean you have to put up with things that hurt you.*

## 7. Letting Go of Family Guilt

*Let's be real: family guilt is real—whether it's guilt about not visiting enough, not meeting their expectations, or feeling like you're not enough. It can weigh so heavy on you, almost like you're constantly failing them. The truth is, you're allowed to not care about that guilt.*

*You are not responsible for their happiness or for making them proud all the time. You can still love them, but you don't need to be their emotional caretaker. You have your own life to live, your own happiness to protect. It's okay to say, "I can't do that right now," or, "I need to take care of myself." It doesn't mean you're abandoning them—it means you're learning to put yourself first so that you don't burn out trying to make everyone else happy.*

## 8. Finding Your Own Space in the Family

*Family dynamics can be a lot—sometimes there's drama, unresolved issues, and patterns that are hard to break. The art of not caring in this context means choosing your role in the family carefully. You don't have to be a part of every argument, carry every burden, or be the one who constantly fixes everything.*

*Loving your family doesn't mean absorbing all their chaos or emotional baggage. It's about finding your space and knowing when to step back for your own well-being. If a family member is constantly draining you or pulling you into their drama, it's okay to say, "This is not my fight" or "I need to take a break from this." You can love them from a distance and still be there for them in ways that don't compromise your own peace.*

*You get to decide what role you play in your family. You don't have to be the problem-solver, the mediator, or the emotional punching bag. Loving your family sometimes means knowing when to step away and protect yourself. And that's a healthy, necessary thing to do.*

## 9. Sometimes, You Have to Care Less

*One of the toughest things about family is realizing that sometimes, you need to care a little less to actually be able to care in the right way. We often think that love means constantly giving, always being available, and making sure everyone else is okay—even if it means neglecting our own needs. But here's the thing: if you're pouring from an empty cup, eventually, there's nothing left to give.*

*The art of not caring here means recognizing that it's okay to pull back sometimes. That doesn't mean you don't love them—it means you're learning to take care of your own needs first. If you're always trying to solve everyone's problems, it can drain you, and you'll lose sight of your own happiness in the process.*

*Sometimes, showing you care means stepping back and letting your family handle their own issues, even if it feels uncomfortable. You're not abandoning them—you're just giving them the space to figure things out on their own, while also taking the time you need for yourself.*

*Loving your family doesn't mean you have to sacrifice your well-being to fix everything. In fact, taking a step back and caring a little less sometimes allows you to be there for them in a more meaningful way, rather than just playing the role of the fixer. It's all about balance.*

*In relationships, the art of not caring isn't about being indifferent or detached—it's about freeing yourself from the unhealthy weight of expectations and fears that keep you from showing up as your true, authentic self. It's not about stopping love; it's about loving with a lighter heart*

*So, when it comes to family, the art of not caring isn't about being cold or distant—it's about loving them without letting their expectations, drama, or guilt overwhelm you. It's about finding that balance where you can love your family for who they are, but still protect your own peace and mental health.*

*It's not selfish to take care of yourself. In fact, it's the healthiest thing you can do—for you and for them.*

## The Logic of Love

*Now, this is the truth, based on logic. But if you ask for my personal opinion, here it is: caring about your family is necessary, and it's a good thing. I have a loving family who cares about me, and it's only natural for me to feel good about them. However, the view I shared earlier about love—that was written from a logical standpoint. If you want my real perspective, it's this:*

*I don't believe in love. Maybe I'm wrong—it's just my own thought, but it feels true to me. Sometimes, it even applies to family. But when it comes to the kind of love that a boy feels for a girl? I don't believe in that at all. I don't know why I feel this way, but maybe* it's because I've never truly felt love or anything close to it. What I think is happening here is more about attraction—or even selective preference—not love.

What people call love follows a pattern: first, you see someone and find them attractive. Then, you start treating them differently from everyone else. It's a simple process, but I don't like it. And as Lord Krishna once said, "No one is truly yours."

Now, this might offend you, but if you compare your so-called love—the attraction or preference you feel—to the connection between Radha and Krishna, you might be the biggest fool of all. I don't know what Radha and Krishna had, but it was something far deeper than what we casually call love. I want to understand that kind of connection, but I know this much: what most people call love is not it.

This is my view of love and the reason I don't believe in it. I don't feel what others feel, and maybe I never will. In this way, I know I am different from most people.

That said, I will admit one truth: there was a time in my life when I was attracted to a girl. It was just attraction, nothing more. Maybe that's when I realized that I can't experience love the way others do—or maybe I never will. It's just not in me.

*If you want a better understanding of my perspective on love, I highly recommend reading Vinland Saga. It's a manga that completely changed my view on the subject. There's a deep conversation between a prince and a priest in the third volume that really made me think—made me question if we are all just living in an illusion. I personally request you to read Vinland Saga because it is a beautiful masterpiece, and I guarantee that whoever starts it will not be the same person by the time they finish.*

*But back to the topic at hand—love is simply not my thing. Maybe in the future, I will understand it better, and when that day comes, I will share what I've learned. But for now, keep this in mind: from my perspective, the love people speak of never truly existed in the first place. I won't say more about it, but to help you understand my thoughts better, I'll explain through a short story.*

### Was It Ever Love?

*Aarav used to believe in forever.*

*When he was with Meera, everything felt right. She was his first real love, the one who made him believe in all those silly romantic movie lines. They would stay up all night talking about their dreams, their future, even the names of their kids. He thought love meant always—that once you found your person, they were yours for life.*

*But forever didn't last.*

*One day, Meera left. No big fight, no betrayal—just quiet, slow-growing distance. And then, nothing. Aarav was heartbroken. He told himself he'd never love anyone like that again. He couldn't. Love wasn't supposed to end.*

*But then came Aisha.*

*She was nothing like Meera. Her laugh was louder, her touch warmer. She saw him in ways Meera never did. And suddenly, everything that used to hurt... didn't hurt anymore. The love he swore was irreplaceable... was replaced.*

*That's when the thought hit him—if I could love again, did I ever really love Meera? If love could change faces, change hearts, was it ever real in the first place?*

*And if he truly loved Aisha now... would he feel the same way about someone else, someday?*

*Maybe love wasn't what he thought it was. Maybe it wasn't forever. Maybe it was just a feeling that came and went, like a season.*

*Or maybe, just maybe... love was never real at all.*

*I don't know much about love, but I remember a Pakistani poet once said:*
*"What kind of love do you have if you can leave it? And if you can leave it, was it ever love?"*

*At the same time, Keanu Reeves once said:*
*"If you're a lover, you gotta be a fighter. Because if you don't fight for your love, what kind of love do you have?"*

*Maybe love is something I simply don't understand. But if I have to believe in love, then what most people experience is not love at all. Like Aarav's story, it's just a game. In my case, I don't feel anything like Keanu Reeves described, and I don't believe in this Gen Z version of love that Aarav's story represents.*

*So, this is my perspective on love. And in my own way, I believe I am right about it. If you want to believe in love, believe in it. If you don't, then don't.*

*Because, in the end—I don't care.*

*And that's the whole point.*

**Chapter Summary : Love, Relationships, and the Art of Not Caring**

**1. Love Doesn't Mean Possession**

*True love is about trust and freedom, not control. When you try to "own" someone, you create a relationship built on fear and dependency rather than genuine connection. Love should empower, not restrict. Letting go of the need to possess someone allows for a more authentic and fulfilling bond.*

**2. Let Go of Expectations**

*Rigid expectations create frustration and disappointment. Love should not be forced into a perfect mold. Instead of dictating how a relationship should unfold, embrace its natural flow. Accept your partner as they are, not as you imagine they should be. Releasing unrealistic expectations allows* relationships to thrive without unnecessary pressure.

## 3. Self-Love Comes First

You cannot give your best to a relationship if you are emotionally drained. Prioritizing self-care is not selfish—it strengthens your ability to love others in a healthy way. A relationship should complement your life, not define it. When you cultivate self-love, you bring confidence and stability into your connections rather than dependency.

## 4. Honest Communication Over Mind Games

Mind games and passive-aggressive behavior only breed confusion and resentment. The art of not caring means saying what you mean and meaning what you say. Open, honest communication fosters trust and clarity, while emotional manipulation only leads to unnecessary drama. Speak directly and expect the same in return.

## 5. Stop Fearing Loss

Love should not be rooted in the fear of losing someone. If a person is meant to stay, they will. If they leave, it is not a personal failure—it is simply the end of a chapter. Accepting that relationships have natural lifespans helps you appreciate love in the *present rather than clinging to it out of fear.*

## 6. Family Love Without Self-Sacrifice

*Loving your family does not mean carrying their burdens as your own. Setting boundaries is essential to maintaining your well-being. You can care for them without losing yourself in their stress, guilt, or expectations. Healthy family relationships are built on mutual respect, not self-sacrifice.*

## 7. Sometimes, You Have to Care Less

*Over-caring can drain you. Not every issue requires your emotional investment. Learning when to step back allows you to preserve your peace while still being present. Whether it's family drama or a toxic relationship, sometimes caring less is the healthiest choice.*

## 8. The Logic of Love vs. Personal Belief

*From a logical standpoint, love may be a mix of attraction and preference rather than something eternal. The story of Aarav questions whether love is real if it can be replaced. The author personally does not believe in romantic love as an absolute truth but acknowledges that others may see it differently.*

## Final Thoughts

*Love and relationships should enrich your life, not control it. The art of not caring is not about detachment but about letting go of fear, control, and unrealistic expectations. When you free yourself from these burdens, love becomes lighter, more natural, and truly fulfilling.*

## CHAPTER FIVE

# MASTERING SOCIAL DETACHMENT

## *Friendships: Detaching Without Losing Connection*

*Hello, humans! Today, I want to talk about friendships and the delicate balance of detaching without losing connection.*

*So, what is friendship? In simple terms, friendship is something that gives you hope, support, and helps solve your problems. But is every friendship like this all the time? Does every friend you make bring you peace and positivity? No, and that's the reality we need to accept.*

*What should we do when a friendship becomes one-sided or emotionally draining? The simple answer is to leave spaces that no longer serve you. But is it always right to walk away? Wouldn't that hurt someone? That's a valid concern, and that's where emotional detachment with balance comes into play.*

*The key is to assess the situation. For example, if a friend consistently dismisses your presence, doesn't give you the respect or consideration you deserve, and only uses you as an emotional dumping ground, then the best thing to do is walk away. Don't overthink it—just let go. After all, why should you care about someone who doesn't care about you? Why invest energy into a person who wouldn't do the same for you? As a famous Bollywood actor once said in a podcast, "Don't sit at a table where you are not respected." And that's the truth—leave behind those who don't deserve your presence.*

*But what if the friend does care about you? In such cases, instead of completely detaching, set healthy boundaries. If you have your own overwhelming problems and aren't in a position to help them, be honest about it. Don't hesitate to express your limits.*

***Example:*** *You have a friend who constantly complains about their problems but never takes advice or makes changes. Instead of getting emotionally drained trying to fix their issues, listen without absorbing their negativity. Set boundaries by saying, "I understand you're going through a lot, but I don't have the energy to keep discussing this. Let's talk about something else."*

*Friendship is about mutual support and respect. If it's one-sided, draining, or toxic, don't hesitate to detach. But when it's genuine, set boundaries to maintain balance while keeping the connection alive.*

**In my personal life, I don't give many people the title of 'friend.' But when I do, it's because I know they are good for me. Simply put, I only expect from someone what they are capable of giving in return.**

*I believe in choosing fewer people—only those who truly deserve it. Because at the end of the day, I am my own company. It's simple: choose less, but choose wisely.*

### Family: Setting Boundaries Without Guilt

*Family comes with expectations—sometimes spoken, sometimes not. They might have strong opinions about your career, relationships, or how you should live your life. And while their intentions may be good, their expectations can feel like a heavy burden, making it difficult to stay true to yourself.*

*Setting boundaries doesn't mean you don't love or respect your family. It simply means you are prioritizing your own well-being and choices.*

*Example: Your family insists that you follow a certain career path or adhere to traditions you don't connect with. You feel the pressure, the weight of their disappointment looming over you. Instead of arguing or justifying yourself, you take a deep breath and calmly say:*
*"I appreciate your concern, but I need to make decisions that align with what feels right for me. Let's respect each other's perspectives."*

*They may push back. They may try to guilt you or make you question your choices. But here's the truth: their expectations do not define your life. You can listen, acknowledge their feelings, and still stand firm in your decisions.*

*Emotional detachment doesn't mean shutting people out; it means recognizing that you don't need their approval to live a fulfilling life. You are allowed to make choices that serve you—even if they don't understand them. The sooner you embrace that, the freer you'll feel*

## Social Circles: Avoiding Emotional Exhaustion

*At some point, we've all felt it—the invisible obligation to say yes. Yes to plans, yes to events, yes to things we don't even enjoy. Not because we want to, but because we feel like we have to. The fear of disappointing others, of being left out, or of seeming like we don't care keeps us trapped in a cycle of social exhaustion.*

*But here's something we rarely stop to consider: constantly saying yes to everyone else often means saying no to ourselves. No to rest. No to peace. No to doing what actually makes us happy.*

*So why do we do it? Because we've been conditioned to believe that declining an invitation is rude or selfish. That we owe everyone a reason, an excuse, a valid explanation. But the truth is, we don't.*

***Example:*** *You're in a group chat, and the usual weekend plans are being thrown around. You're exhausted. Work, life, responsibilities—everything has drained you, and all you want is a quiet night to yourself. But then comes the pressure: "Come on, you never come out anymore!" or "Just this once, we miss you!"*

*So, you start debating: Do I just suck it up and go? Do I make up an excuse? Do I over-explain why I need to stay home?*

*No. You don't. Instead, you simply say:*

*"I won't be able to make it, but I hope you all have fun!"*

*That's it. No long explanations. No justifications. No guilt.*

*And here's the best part—most people won't even question it. They'll move on with their plans, and you'll finally have the space to do what you need. And if someone does push? That's a sign that they might not fully understand your boundaries. It's not the same for everyone—sometimes, people genuinely don't grasp your situation. They may think they're helping when, in reality, they're adding pressure, like a brother or a close friend who just wants you to be involved.*

*The key here isn't just learning to say no. It's understanding that your well-being matters just as much as everyone else's. You're not a bad friend for prioritizing yourself. The people who genuinely care about you will get it. And those who don't? Well, maybe it's time to rethink why you're so worried about their opinion in the first place.*

*Setting boundaries in social circles isn't about shutting people out—it's about making sure you don't shut yourself out in the process*

**Workplace: Detaching from Drama**

*Office politics. Gossip. The never-ending cycle of who said what, who's getting promoted, and who's secretly feuding with whom. It's easy to get pulled into the drama—sometimes, it even feels like you have to participate just to fit in.*

*But here's the thing: engaging in workplace gossip rarely benefits you. More often than not, it drains your energy, creates unnecessary tension, and can even backfire. The more you invest in these conversations, the more you risk being associated with negativity.*

***Example:*** *You're sitting in the break room, and your coworkers start venting about office politics. They exchange whispers about management, share complaints about colleagues, and look to you for input. The pressure to chime in is real—you don't want to seem standoffish, but you also don't want to get sucked in.*

*So instead of engaging emotionally, you take a different approach. You acknowledge their words neutrally with a simple,* **"That's interesting,"** *and then smoothly redirect the conversation. Maybe you shift the focus to a neutral topic or excuse yourself entirely.*

*This subtle response keeps you from being dragged into negativity while maintaining your professionalism. Over time, people will recognize that you're not someone who fuels drama—and that's a reputation worth having.*

*At the end of the day, protecting your peace at work isn't just about avoiding conflict. It's about recognizing that your energy is limited, and wasting it on office politics doesn't get you closer to your goals. The less you engage in unnecessary drama, the more time and focus you'll have for what actually matters—your growth, your work, and your own peace of mind.*

*And this doesn't just apply to the workplace. **Whether it's family gatherings, friend groups, or online discussions, the same principle holds true—detaching from drama keeps you in control of your energy and your emotions.** You don't have to play a role in every conversation, and you don't have to let other people's negativity become yours.*

### *Social Media: Detaching from Opinions*

*Social media has turned the world into one big comment section. Everyone has an opinion, and thanks to the internet, they have a platform to share it—whether you asked for it or not.*

*You could post something harmless, something meaningful, or even something completely random,* and before you know it, someone is there to criticize, mock, or argue. It's almost inevitable. But here's what most people forget: **just because someone has an opinion about you doesn't mean it matters.**

Yet, this is where many people get trapped. They let a stranger's words ruin their mood. They feel the need to defend themselves, explain their perspective, or prove something to someone they don't even know. They replay the comment in their mind, overanalyze it, and suddenly, a few meaningless words from an online stranger have taken up valuable space in their head.

But here's the truth: **their opinion doesn't change your reality.**

**Example:** You share something online—maybe a personal thought, a creative project, or even just a funny meme. A notification pops up. Someone left a rude comment, criticized your opinion, or tried to start an argument.

At that moment, you have two choices:

1.
    Engage, defend yourself, and waste energy on someone who probably won't change their mind.

2.

*Detach, remind yourself that their words don't define you, and move on.*

*Instead of getting caught up in the negativity, you pause and think: **"Their opinion doesn't change my reality."***

*Then, you do what serves your peace—ignore it, delete it, mute them, or even laugh it off. Whatever keeps your energy intact. Because the moment you stop giving power to negativity, it loses its hold over you.*

*This isn't about ignoring all feedback. Constructive criticism can be valuable. But there's a difference between healthy dialogue and pointless negativity. And if someone's only contribution to your life is criticism without substance, they were never worth your time to begin with.*

*At the end of the day, social media is just a tool. It's not real life. How much control it has over your emotions is entirely up to you. And the more you learn to detach from random opinions, the more peace you'll find—both online and in the real world.*

**"The Hidden Rule of Effortless Friendships"**

*What if the secret to happy, drama-free relationships wasn't about finding the right people—but about understanding how to connect with them the right way?*

*Most people believe that deep friendships require constant togetherness, shared experiences, and an unspoken rule that a best friend should always be there for everything. But expectations like these can turn friendships into obligations rather than natural, fulfilling connections.*

*The truth is, no single person can be everything to you. People have different interests, different ways of expressing care, and different personal limits. Trying to fit all your social needs into just one relationship only creates pressure—both for you and for them. But when you learn to appreciate people for what they bring to your life without forcing them into roles they weren't meant for, friendships become lighter, more natural, and free of unnecessary disappointment.*

*Understanding this simple rule changes everything. It makes relationships more effortless, removes unnecessary tension, and allows genuine connections to thrive. Because in the end, friendships aren't about possession or expectation—they're about connection, respect, and the freedom to let people be who they truly are.*

*Ayan and Rohan were two friends, but they had completely different ways of forming relationships. Ayan believed in spending time with people based on shared interests, while Rohan thought true friendship meant doing everything with just one person.*

*Ayan was easygoing and practical. If he wanted to watch a movie, he'd call up Arjun, his movie-buff friend, and they'd have deep discussions about the plot afterward. When he felt like playing football, he wouldn't drag Arjun along—he'd hit up Kabir, who shared his love for sports. To Ayan, it just made sense. Different people had different interests, and he enjoyed each friendship for what it was, without forcing anyone into things they didn't enjoy.*

*It wasn't just about hobbies either. When Ayan needed someone to talk to about life and deeper thoughts, he'd meet Meera, who always had great insights. But when he just wanted to goof around and laugh, he'd hang out with Riya, the funniest person he knew. This way, he never felt like he was expecting too much from any one person. And because of that, his friendships stayed light, natural, and fulfilling.*

*Rohan, on the other hand, saw things differently. He believed that a real best friend should do everything together. For him, that person was Sameer. No matter what Rohan wanted to do—watch a movie, play football, go on a road trip—Sameer was his go-to. Even if Sameer wasn't into movies or sports, Rohan would insist, expecting him to tag along no matter what.*

*At first, Sameer tried to keep up. He sat through movies he didn't care about and played football even though he wasn't athletic. But over time, he started feeling drained. One day, when Rohan excitedly planned a weekend trip and Sameer said, "Hey man, I think I just need some time to myself this weekend," Rohan felt completely let down. He had poured everything into one friendship, expecting Sameer to always be there, but in the end, he was left disappointed and alone.*

*That's when it hit him—maybe he was putting too much pressure on one person. Maybe friendships weren't about sticking to just one person for everything, but about embracing different people for different moments.*

*Ayan, who spread his connections naturally, always had someone to enjoy life with. Rohan, who put all his expectations on one person, ended up feeling hurt. In friendships, balance is key. No one person can be everything for you, and when you accept that, relationships feel lighter, happier, and more real.*

*Evry one is not like you they have there different life prospective and different way of doing things so just let them be themselves and don't put to mutch hope And at some point, you are alone, so you have to accept it.*

*People will come and go, connections will shift, and even the closest bonds will change with time. No one is meant to be everything for you, just as you can't be everything for them. The moment you stop expecting permanence, friendships feel lighter, and relationships feel less like obligations. Let people be who they are, without forcing them into roles they were never meant to fill. And most importantly, remember this—at some point, you are alone, and that's not a tragedy; it's just life. The sooner you accept it, the freer you become .*

**Chapter Summary :**

**1. Friendships & Detachment**

*Not every friendship is worth holding onto. Some connections become one-sided, draining, or even toxic over time. Detachment doesn't mean being cold or indifferent; it means recognizing when a friendship is no longer serving you. Instead of clinging to people out of habit or obligation, focus on mutual connections that uplift and support you. Real friends respect your boundaries and don't make you feel exhausted.*

## 2. Family & Boundaries

*Family is important, but it should never come at the cost of your mental and emotional well-being. Many people feel obligated to tolerate toxic behaviors just because they come from family members. However, love and respect don't mean sacrificing your peace. It's okay to set boundaries, say no, and protect your own happiness—even if that means disappointing others. Healthy family relationships thrive on mutual understanding, not guilt or control.*

## 3. Social Circles & Emotional Exhaustion

*Not every invitation requires a "yes." Many of us feel pressured to be social, to attend every gathering, or to constantly engage with others. But constantly saying yes can drain your energy and leave you feeling overwhelmed. Learning to say "no" without guilt—or without over-explaining—is essential to maintaining emotional balance. Your time and energy are valuable, and it's okay to be selective about where you invest them.*

## 4. Workplace & Drama

*The workplace can be a breeding ground for gossip, unnecessary drama, and toxic competition. Getting caught up in office politics only adds stress and distracts from what actually matters—your own professional growth. The best approach is to stay neutral, avoid unnecessary conflicts, and focus on your own goals. When you stop caring about workplace drama, you gain a sense of control and peace in your professional life.*

## 5. Social Media & Opinions

*The internet is filled with people who love to argue, judge, and criticize. But here's the truth: other people's opinions of you are none of your business. Engaging in pointless online debates or trying to prove yourself to strangers is a waste of time. Detach from negativity and focus on what truly adds value to your life. Your self-worth should never be dependent on likes, comments, or external validation.*

## 6. Effortless Friendships

*Expecting one person to fulfill all your emotional needs is unrealistic. No single friendship or relationship can be everything to you—and that's okay. Instead of forcing people to fit into your expectations, appreciate them for what they naturally bring into your life. Some friends are great for deep conversations, while others are perfect for lighthearted fun. Understanding this makes relationships feel more natural and fulfilling.*

## 7. The Reality of Change

*Friendships, relationships, and personal dynamics evolve over time. People grow, circumstances shift, and sometimes, bonds weaken. Instead of resisting change or mourning the loss of what used to be, embrace the natural flow of life. Holding onto the past only creates unnecessary suffering. Letting go of attachments and allowing relationships to evolve organically makes them feel lighter and more authentic.*

## 8. Embracing Solitude

*At some point in life, you will find yourself alone, and that's not a tragedy—it's a reality. Many people fear solitude, but in truth, being alone doesn't mean being lonely. When you stop fearing isolation and start embracing it, you gain true freedom. You realize that your happiness isn't dependent on others but comes from within. Learning to enjoy your own company is one of the most empowering things you can do.*

## CHAPTER SIX

# THE RELAPSE –
# WHEN YOU START
# CARING AGAIN

*I want to be real with you.*

*You've been practicing the art of not caring. You've stopped letting other people's opinions control your vibe. You've let go of judgment and done things that feel true to you. You've taken the "One Day" theory and made it work—you've been authentic, unapologetic, and free.*

*But then... it happened.*

*It wasn't a dramatic fall. You didn't suddenly start caring about everything at once. But slowly, quietly, without even realizing it—**you slipped.***

*It could have been a comment someone made that hit a little too close to home. Or maybe you saw a picture of your friend's perfect life and suddenly felt like yours wasn't quite up to par. Maybe you found yourself scrolling through social media, comparing your achievements to others', and questioning if you were enough. Or maybe you heard someone talking behind your back, and just like that, the familiar feeling of insecurity crept in.*

*I get it.* **You started caring again.**

*And here's the truth—**it's normal**. Relapse is a part of the process. Caring less isn't a switch you flick and then forget about. It's a practice. A constant, evolving challenge. So let's talk about it. Let's break down **The Relapse** and how to handle it when it hits.*

**It Starts Subtle**

*The relapse doesn't come crashing down on you like a storm. It starts slow, almost unnoticeable. It's like a shadow that creeps up on you, silently changing your mindset. At first, you don't notice. Maybe you're out with friends, and you find yourself overthinking everything you say or do, trying to fit into their expectations. You start second-guessing yourself. Maybe someone mentioned your passion for something they didn't quite understand, and suddenly, that seed of doubt is planted.*

*You look in the mirror and wonder if your clothes are "too weird" again. You scroll through your phone, searching for validation that you didn't know you needed. You start caring about who liked your post or how many people watched your story. All of a sudden, it feels like you're back in the old habit of trying to impress everyone around you.*

*This is what I mean when I say relapse isn't dramatic. It's subtle. It sneaks up on you like a quiet friend, sitting next to you when you least expect it. But don't freak out.* **Recognizing it early is half the battle.**

### My Own Relapse – The Moment I Cared Again

*I'll be honest with you—I've had moments where I completely slipped back into the cycle of caring too much. There was a time when I had just experienced one of the most freeing days of my life. I went to a music studio, wore my favorite white anime t-shirt, played guitar for hours, watched a movie alone in the theater, and just did me.*

*But a few days later, something changed.*

*I was walking down the street, feeling high on life, when I overheard a conversation. Two people were talking about how "pathetic" they thought it was when people go out to the movies alone. They were laughing about it, saying that people who do that must have no friends.*

*And for a split second, something shifted inside me. I felt that old, familiar sting of insecurity. Wait... Am I that person?*

*It was such a small moment, but it hit me hard. The doubt, the fear, the need for validation from others—it all came flooding back. I started questioning my decision to watch movies alone, wondering if it was "weird" or if I was just being anti-social. And in that moment, I slipped.*

*But here's the thing: I didn't stay there. I caught myself before it went too far. I realized this was just a relapse. I wasn't a failure. I was just human. I reminded myself that I wasn't living for anyone but me, and that was enough.*

## *How to Spot the Warning Signs*

*So, how do you know when you're falling back into old habits? When you've started to care too much again, how can you spot it early?*

- **You're constantly adjusting yourself.** *Maybe you're trying to fit into a mold that you know isn't yours. You're putting on a mask to please others, changing how you act, dress, or speak just to fit in. This is the first sign that you're slipping.*

- **You start seeking external validation.** *You might find yourself refreshing your phone, checking for likes, comments, or shares, even when it doesn't matter to you. Or you start questioning your worth based on how many people support you. That's the red flag.*

- **You shrink to avoid discomfort.** *If you find yourself laughing at jokes you don't find funny, agreeing with things you don't believe in, or saying "yes" when you want to say "no," it's a sign you're giving away your power. You're trying to avoid conflict and make others happy, even at the cost of your own happiness.*

## The Truth About Why You Relapse

*Here's what's going on: the reason you slip back into caring is that it's been a part of your routine for so long. You've been conditioned to look for approval from others. We grow up with societal pressure telling us that we need to fit in, be "normal," and follow the rules. It's drilled into us that our worth is tied to the approval of others. So when we stop caring and start living authentically, it feels like we're swimming against the current.*

*Think about it like this: You've spent years trying to be accepted. Even if you've learned the art of not caring, your mind is still wired to seek out that approval. So, when you face a situation where you feel "judged" again, it's natural to slip back into old patterns of caring. The difference is now you can catch it.*

## How to Clean Up the Mess and Bounce Back

*Now that we've discussed why you relapse, let's talk about how to get back on track. Here's what you can do when you feel yourself slipping back into those old habits:*

## 1. Pause and Reflect

*Take a step back. When you feel yourself slipping, pause. Don't just continue down the road of self-doubt. Reflect on why you're feeling this way. Is it because you truly care, or are you seeking validation? This moment of awareness is the first step to reclaiming your authenticity.*

## 2. Journal It Out

*Write down your feelings. What triggered your relapse? What made you start caring again? Write down the story of what happened, and reflect on the emotions that came up. Writing helps you separate your feelings from the situation and gain perspective.*

## 3. Take Small Steps to Regain Control

*Sometimes, it's the small, simple actions that help us regain control. For me, when I felt my relapse creeping in, I reminded myself of the One Day Theory. I took an hour for myself to do something that brought me pure joy—whether it was playing the guitar, going for a walk, or just watching a movie. It's all about taking moments to reconnect with your true self.*

## The Relapse Isn't Defeat – It's a Step in the Process

*Remember: relapse isn't failure. It's part of the process. You've been rewiring your mind to stop seeking validation from others, and that's no easy task. But every time you slip and catch yourself, you get better at it. You'll learn to recognize the patterns faster, and you'll bounce back quicker each time. It's all about growth.*

## Final Thoughts – Healing Isn't Linear

*The path to not caring is a journey. It's a practice, not a one-time achievement. Just like any skill you develop, it takes time. And sometimes you'll slip. That's okay. You'll learn to bounce back. You'll learn to stay true to yourself, even when it feels uncomfortable.*

*So, when you relapse, don't be hard on yourself. Don't let it drag you down. Instead, use it as a reminder that healing isn't linear. It's a cycle, and every time you go through it, you grow stronger.*

*The only thing that matters is you.* **Keep practicing.**

## Chapter 7: Becoming the Villain (in Their Story)

*Here's the thing: when you stop caring and start choosing yourself, there will be people who won't like it. In fact, you might find that you'll become the "villain" in their story. And you know what?* **That's okay.**

*Let me explain. The moment you start setting boundaries, being unapologetically you, and making decisions that are in your best interest—other people will start to label you. They'll say you're selfish. They'll say you've changed. They'll talk behind your back. They'll call you cold, distant, or "too much" because you're no longer playing by their rules.*

*But here's the truth:* **You don't need their approval.** *You don't need to play the role they've assigned to you. You are the hero of your own story, and sometimes, that means you have to become the villain in someone else's.*

### The Villain Archetype

*In any good story, there's always a villain. They're the ones who stand in the way of the protagonist, challenge their beliefs, and force them to grow. But here's the thing: the villain isn't always the bad guy. Often, they're the ones who force the hero to step up, to stand firm, and to take control of their destiny.*

*When you stop caring and start choosing yourself, you become the villain in someone's story. The difference is, you're not doing it out of malice. You're doing it because you've decided that your happiness and peace are more important than living for the approval of others.*

## The Power of Setting Boundaries

*One of the hardest things to do when you start caring less is setting boundaries. People don't like boundaries. They want you to be available whenever they need you. They want you to do things their way. But setting boundaries is essential if you're going to stay true to yourself.*

*You'll find that as you start setting boundaries, people might call you selfish. They might say, "You've changed." They might guilt-trip you into doing things you don't want to do. But remember this: **Boundaries aren't selfish; they're necessary.***

## Let Them Misunderstand You

*One of the hardest things you'll face in this journey is being misunderstood. When you stop caring about what others think and start living for yourself, some people will not get it. And that's okay. You're not here to be liked by everyone. You're here to live your truth.*

Let people misunderstand you. Let them call you selfish or distant. Because at the end of the day, **you're choosing your freedom.** You're choosing peace. You're choosing to live your life on your own terms.

## Being the Villain Is a Sign of Strength

Here's the truth: Sometimes being the villain in their story is the price of being the hero in yours. It's not about being cruel or vindictive. It's about putting yourself first. It's about recognizing that you can't make everyone happy, and you shouldn't try.

Choosing yourself may make others uncomfortable, but it doesn't make you a bad person. It makes you strong. It makes you resilient. It makes you a hero in your own life.

## Final Thoughts: Hero of Your Story

You are the hero of your story. And sometimes, to be that hero, you have to become the villain in someone else's.

So, embrace it. Set those boundaries. Make decisions that align with your values, not others' expectations. And don't be afraid to let go of relationships or *situations that no longer serve you. You have to choose yourself first, and if that makes you the villain in someone's story, then so be it.*

*Because you are worthy of happiness, peace, and freedom. And that's worth being the villain for.*

*Chapter Summary:*

*Relapsing Is Normal: Even after practicing emotional detachment, you may occasionally start caring again—about people's opinions, validation, or fitting in. This is a natural part of growth, not a failure.*

*It Starts Subtly: Relapse often begins quietly—through small insecurities, comparisons, or the need for external approval. Recognizing these early signs is key to stopping the spiral.*

*Personal Story of Slipping: The author shares a moment when outside judgment triggered self-doubt, despite feeling previously free. This shows how deeply conditioned approval-seeking behavior is.*

*Warning Signs to Watch: Signs of relapse include adjusting your identity to please others, craving likes or compliments, and shrinking yourself to avoid conflict.*

*Why We Relapse: Society conditions us from a young age to seek acceptance. Relapsing means old mental habits are resurfacing—not that you've failed.*

*Bouncing Back: You can recover from a relapse by pausing to reflect, journaling your feelings, and reconnecting with things that make you feel authentically you.*

*Becoming the Villain Is Power: When you prioritize yourself, set boundaries, or stop people-pleasing, some will label you as selfish or distant. Let them. You're just choosing yourself.*

*Hero of Your Own Story: Being the "villain" in someone else's story is often necessary to be the hero in your own. Choosing peace, freedom, and truth—even at the cost of being misunderstood—is real strength.*

# VITAMIN N – THE POWER OF SAYING NO

## Introduction: The Power of No

*We live in a world that constantly pulls us in different directions. From work commitments to social obligations, it seems there's always someone or something demanding our time, attention, or energy. The word "yes" often slips out of our mouths without us even thinking, as if it's the default response to any request. But what if the true key to mental clarity, emotional well-being, and personal freedom was hiding in one simple word: no?*

*It might sound counterintuitive. After all, we've been taught that saying yes is the polite thing to do. We're encouraged to be accommodating, helpful, and cooperative—to always show up, no matter the cost.*

*Saying yes feels like an act of kindness, a way to keep the peace or prove that we're capable and dependable.*

*But here's the truth: the word "no" is not a villain. It's not selfish. It's not rude. In fact, it's one of the most powerful tools we have for self-care and personal growth. When you learn to say no, you begin to take control of your life, stop letting others dictate your time, and focus on what truly matters to you.*

*Saying no is an act of empowerment. It's a boundary that you set to protect your energy, your time, and your well-being. And yes, it can feel uncomfortable at first. You might worry about disappointing others or feeling guilty for turning someone down. But if you don't make space for yourself, if you don't protect your time, no one else will.*

*In this chapter, we'll explore why learning to say no is one of the most liberating skills you can develop. We'll look at the psychology behind our need to please, the toll saying yes all the time can take on us, and how saying no is actually a form of self-love and respect.*

*So, let's take a deep breath and step into the world of Vitamin N. Trust me—your life will never be the same after you embrace the power of no.*

## 2. Why We Struggle to Say No

*For many of us, saying no feels like a monumental task. It's as if we've been conditioned to say yes to everything that comes our way, no matter how much it drains us. But why is it so hard to turn down a request, even when we know it's not in our best interest?*

*At the core of it, the struggle to say no often comes from a deep-seated fear of disappointing others. We fear that by saying no, we'll be perceived as rude, selfish, or unkind. We might worry about hurting someone's feelings or damaging a relationship. The truth is, saying no can feel like we're rejecting someone or their needs, which makes it incredibly uncomfortable.*

*It doesn't help that society reinforces these expectations. From a young age, we're taught to be people-pleasers. We're praised for being helpful, kind, and considerate of others. "Don't be selfish," we hear repeatedly. In this context, saying no can feel like an act of defiance, a break from the norm. And let's face it: when you grow up hearing that being kind means saying yes all the time, it becomes ingrained in how we approach the world.*

*The fear of judgment also plays a big role in our struggle to say no. Many of us worry about what others might think. "What if they think I'm not a good friend? What if they think I'm lazy or unhelpful?" These thoughts run through our minds, paralyzing us and making it difficult to set clear boundaries. The fear of rejection can be so strong that we're willing to sacrifice our own needs to avoid conflict or discomfort.*

*Additionally, there's the underlying fear of missing out (FOMO). We've all been there—someone invites us to an event, and our first instinct is to say yes because we don't want to miss out on a fun time or an opportunity to connect. But this kind of thinking puts us in a constant state of overcommitment. Instead of prioritizing what truly matters, we end up spreading ourselves too thin, always chasing the next thing without ever being truly present.*

*It's also easy to fall into the trap of over-explaining. When we do muster the courage to say no, we often feel the need to justify our decision with lengthy excuses, as if we need permission to prioritize ourselves. In reality, we shouldn't have to explain ourselves to anyone. Our time, our energy, and our boundaries are ours to protect.*

*So, why do we keep saying yes when we know it's not always in our best interest? The short answer is fear—fear of judgment, fear of missing out, and fear of disappointing others. But the longer answer is that saying yes has become a habit, and breaking that habit takes time, courage, and practice.*

### 3. The Hidden Cost of Saying Yes All the Time

*We all know that saying yes feels good in the moment. It makes us feel helpful, liked, and needed. But what we often overlook are the hidden costs of constantly putting others' needs before our own. In the long run, saying yes too often can lead to emotional burnout, physical exhaustion, and a sense of resentment that can seep into our relationships.*

*One of the most damaging costs is **burnout**. When we're constantly saying yes to everything, we spread ourselves so thin that we lose sight of our own well-being. Over time, this can leave us feeling drained, overwhelmed, and completely out of touch with our own desires and needs. It's easy to get caught in a cycle of giving and doing for others until we hit a breaking point. When this happens, we're no longer able to be the best version of ourselves, whether it's at work, in our relationships, or in our own personal pursuits.*

*But burnout isn't the only hidden cost. Constantly saying yes can lead to **resentment**. It's one thing to help others, but when we feel like we're always the one giving, and others are never reciprocating, frustration builds. We might even feel taken advantage of, which can affect our relationships with friends, family, and colleagues. The more we say yes out of obligation, the less meaningful those acts of kindness become. Instead of feeling satisfied by helping, we begin to feel resentful, wishing others would respect our boundaries or offer us the same kindness in return.*

*Over time, this builds a sense of **self-neglect**. We lose sight of what makes us happy, what drives us, and what we want to do with our lives. When we're constantly prioritizing others, we put our own dreams, goals, and passions on the backburner. This can lead to a deep sense of dissatisfaction, as we wake up one day realizing we've lived most of our lives for others, neglecting the things that truly bring us joy. The more we say yes to things that don't align with our values or interests, the more disconnected we become from our true selves.*

*The toll of overcommitting can even extend to our **mental health**. Saying yes all the time often means taking on too much, leaving little time for rest or self-care. Over time, this can increase stress levels, anxiety, and feelings of inadequacy. When we can't meet the expectations we've set for ourselves (or that others have set for us), it chips away at our self-esteem. We start to feel like we're not doing enough, or worse, that we're not enough.*

*And let's not forget about the **impact on our relationships**. Paradoxically, constantly saying yes can actually harm our relationships. While we might think we're being helpful or supportive, we might actually be enabling unhealthy dynamics. By always saying yes, we allow others to become dependent on us, which can lead to imbalanced relationships. People might start expecting us to always be available, which puts undue pressure on us. Eventually, we might feel like we're more of a "resource" to others than a person* *with our own needs and desires.*

*The point is this: saying yes to everything comes at a price. It chips away at our time, energy, and well-being until we're left feeling exhausted, disconnected, and overwhelmed. But here's the kicker—most of the time, the things we say yes to don't even matter as much as we think they do. We give so much of ourselves away to obligations, expectations, and people who may never appreciate the sacrifice.*

*The real cost of saying yes all the time isn't just in our time or energy—it's in the quiet, insidious erosion of who we are and what we stand for. Saying yes to everything means saying no to the things that truly matter: our peace of mind, our self-respect, and our happiness.*

## 4. Saying No as a Form of Self-Love

*We often think of love as something we give to others: affection, kindness, understanding, and support. But self-love is just as important, and it's something that we often overlook. In reality, self-love is not just about pampering yourself or indulging in things you enjoy. It's also about setting boundaries, protecting your peace, and making choices that honor your well-being. And one of the most powerful ways to practice self-love is by saying no.*

*When we say yes to everything, we're neglecting our own needs in favor of others' demands. But when we say no, we're saying "I value myself enough to prioritize my well-being." We're taking a stand for our time, our energy, and our mental space. Saying no is an act of courage—it's the ability to turn down what doesn't serve us, no matter how much pressure we face. In this way, no is a form of protection—a shield against the things that drain us.*

*Think about the last time you said yes to something out of obligation, even though you didn't want to. How did you feel afterward? Maybe you were exhausted, resentful, or even frustrated with yourself for not speaking up. Saying yes when you don't want to is essentially telling yourself that others' needs are more important than your own, that you're not worthy of putting yourself first. But self-love demands the opposite. It's about recognizing that you have the right to say no, to create space for yourself, and to say yes only to what truly aligns with your values.*

*Self-love isn't selfish—it's essential. By saying no, you're honoring your own time, energy, and limits. You're telling yourself that you deserve rest, relaxation, and peace of mind. You're saying that your own happiness matters as much as anyone else's. This doesn't mean that you're abandoning others or being cold—it simply means you're setting healthy boundaries to protect your emotional and physical health.*

*Think of it like this: would you let someone keep taking things from you without ever giving back? Of course not. So why would you keep giving away your time, energy, and emotional labor without considering the cost to yourself? Saying no is about filling your own cup before trying to pour into others. It's about recognizing that in order to truly be there for others, you need to be whole, rested, and energized yourself.*

*Saying no as a form of self-love also means that you're learning to listen to your inner voice. It's the practice of tuning into what you really need, rather than succumbing to external pressures. When you say no, you're giving yourself permission to honor your own intuition and desires. It's a reminder that you don't have to be everything to everyone—just enough for yourself.*

## 5. How to Start Saying No

*Now that we understand why saying no is so important and the costs of not setting boundaries, the next step is learning how to actually start saying no. For many of us, the thought of rejecting someone or turning down a request can feel uncomfortable, even anxiety-inducing. But with a little practice, it becomes easier, and more importantly, it becomes a powerful act of self-care. Here are some practical tips on how to begin saying no in a way that feels empowering, not guilty:*

## 1. Start Small

If saying no feels overwhelming, start with small, low-stakes situations. Practice saying no to minor requests that don't carry too much emotional weight. For example, you might say no to attending a social event you're not interested in or declining an invitation to take on an extra project at work. By gradually building your "no" muscle in these smaller situations, you'll gain confidence to use it in more challenging scenarios.

## 2. Be Direct and Honest

One of the main reasons we struggle with saying no is because we feel the need to explain ourselves or offer lengthy excuses. But the truth is, you don't owe anyone an explanation. Saying no doesn't require you to justify your decision—especially if your reason is simply that it's not the right fit for you. Practice being direct but polite: "I'm going to have to pass on this, but I appreciate you thinking of me." You don't need to go into details or over-explain. A simple, honest no is enough.

## 3. Set Clear Boundaries

The more clearly you communicate your boundaries, the easier it will be to say no when they're crossed. If you know you need time to rest on weekends, or *that you don't want to take on any additional responsibilities at work, make those boundaries clear to others. People are more likely to respect your no if they already know what your limits are. For example, you might say, "I'm not available for work calls after 6 PM" or "I don't take on last-minute plans anymore." Setting expectations upfront helps prevent misunderstandings and makes it easier for others to respect your decision.*

## 4. Don't Feel Guilty

*Guilt is a common emotion when we say no, especially if we're used to saying yes all the time. But here's the thing: you're not being selfish when you say no—you're protecting your time, energy, and mental health. Remind yourself that taking care of yourself benefits everyone in your life. You can't pour from an empty cup. It's okay to prioritize yourself. If guilt arises, acknowledge it, but don't let it dictate your decisions.*

## 5. Practice Saying No in Different Ways

*Sometimes, saying no can be more nuanced than just rejecting a request outright. There are many ways to turn something down politely without feeling harsh or rude. Here are a few examples:*

- 

*The soft no:* "I'd love to, but I can't this time."

- *The postponed no:* "I'm not able to do this now, but maybe we can revisit it later."

- *The redirect no:* "I'm not the best person for this, but I can recommend someone who might be."

These approaches allow you to turn something down while still being kind and respectful. You're asserting your boundaries without feeling like you're being confrontational or inconsiderate.

## 6. Stand Firm, Even if There's Pushback

The first few times you say no, you might encounter resistance. Some people might push back, try to guilt-trip you, or argue with your decision. This is normal, especially if they're used to you always saying yes. Remember, their reaction is not your responsibility. It's okay for people to be disappointed or upset, but that doesn't mean you have to change your decision. Stand firm in your "no," and don't let others' feelings sway you. The more you practice saying no, the more comfortable you'll become with handling resistance.

## 7. Use the Power of No to Protect Your Time

*One of the most valuable resources we have is our time. When you say yes to something, you're essentially saying no to other possibilities—whether it's time for yourself, time to focus on your passions, or time to rest. By learning to say no, you're giving yourself the gift of time. Time to focus on what really matters. Time to create, to recharge, to reflect, or to simply be.*

*Think of saying no as a way to **guard** your time fiercely, the same way you would guard something precious. Time is non-renewable, and once it's gone, you can't get it back. Every time you say yes to something that doesn't align with your goals or values, you're sacrificing precious time that could be spent on things that truly fulfill you.*

## 6. Building a "No" Mindset for Life

*Now that you understand the importance of saying no and how to implement it in your daily life, let's explore how to cultivate a "No" mindset. This mindset isn't just about saying no in individual situations—it's about adopting a perspective that honors your time, energy, and boundaries in all aspects of life. Once you start building a "No" mindset, it becomes easier to navigate the challenges and demands that come your way, and you'll be able to make choices that support your well-being.*

## 1. Recognize Your Value

*The foundation of the "No" mindset is a strong sense of self-worth. When you recognize your value and the importance of protecting your time and energy, saying no becomes much easier. The more you understand that you deserve respect, space, and time to nurture your own goals, the more natural it is to say no without guilt.*

*Think of yourself as a resource—something precious and finite. Just as you wouldn't want to waste your money or your energy on things that don't bring value to your life, you shouldn't waste your time on commitments that drain or deplete you. Your time is the one resource that you can never get back, so it should be treated with care and respect. Recognizing your value allows you to say no without second-guessing your decision.*

## 2. Shift from People-Pleasing to Self-Pleasing

One of the reasons it's hard for many of us to say no is because we fear disappointing others. We're conditioned to believe that we have to constantly please people in order to be liked or accepted. But when you adopt a "No" mindset, you start shifting from people-pleasing to self-pleasing.

*People-pleasing leads to burnout, resentment, and the neglect of your own needs. It's a cycle that robs you of your time, energy, and happiness. But self-pleasing—making choices based on your needs, desires, and values—creates a sense of empowerment. It means prioritizing your well-being, regardless of whether others approve or understand. It's about trusting that when you honor your own needs, you're better equipped to show up for others in a more genuine and sustainable way.*

### 3. Get Comfortable with Discomfort

*Saying no isn't always easy, and you'll likely feel some discomfort along the way. People might push back, question your decision, or even try to make you feel guilty for saying no. That's okay. It's normal to feel discomfort when you start changing long-standing habits or patterns of behavior.*

*However, discomfort doesn't mean you're making the wrong choice. In fact, discomfort is often a sign of growth. It's a sign that you're challenging yourself and stepping outside your comfort zone. The more you practice saying no, the less uncomfortable it will feel. Over time, you'll realize that the discomfort of saying no is much less painful than the regret and burnout that comes from constantly saying yes.*

### 4. Make Saying No a Habit

*The key to building a "No" mindset is repetition. Just like any habit, saying no requires practice. Start by saying no in small situations and gradually work your way up to more challenging scenarios. The more you say no, the easier it becomes to do so without hesitation or guilt.*

*For example, if you're invited to an event you don't want to attend, practice saying no politely and confidently: "I appreciate the invite, but I won't be able to make it." Over time, this simple practice will become second nature. You'll start to recognize opportunities to say no in situations where you used to say yes out of obligation.*

*As you build this habit, you'll begin to notice a shift in how you view your time and energy. Instead of seeing them as resources to be freely given away, you'll start seeing them as things to be carefully protected and invested in.*

### 5. Say No to Fear of Missing Out (FOMO)

*In today's world, the fear of missing out (FOMO) is a constant pressure. We're bombarded with invitations, opportunities, and experiences, all vying for our attention. It's easy to think that if we say no, we'll miss out on something important or fun. But the reality is, saying no can actually lead to a deeper sense of fulfillment.*

*When you say no to things that don't align with your priorities, you're saying yes to things that truly matter. You're investing your time in activities that bring you joy, help you grow, and contribute to your well-being. Saying no to FOMO means acknowledging that your time is limited, and you want to spend it in ways that truly resonate with you. It's about choosing quality over quantity—choosing depth over breadth.*

## 6. Embrace the Power of No

*Ultimately, building a "No" mindset is about embracing the power of choice. Saying no isn't about rejecting others—it's about rejecting the things that don't serve you. It's about standing firm in your convictions, knowing that by saying no, you're choosing yourself and your well-being. Over time, this mindset will not only make saying no easier but also empower you to make decisions that align with your true self.*

*The power of no is about being deliberate with your energy and your time. It's about creating space for the things that matter most. And when you live from this place of conscious choice, you'll find that your life becomes richer, more fulfilling, and more aligned with your deepest desires.*

## 7. Embracing the Freedom of No

*Saying no isn't just about rejecting requests, invitations, or opportunities. It's about embracing the ultimate freedom of living on your own terms. The power to say no is a tool that allows you to shape your life the way you want it—on your schedule, aligned with your values, and filled with the people and activities that actually bring you joy and fulfillment.*

*At its core, saying no is not about shutting others down—it's about opening up space for what truly matters to you. When you start saying no, you unlock a new level of freedom, one where you can fully embrace who you are, what you want, and how you want to live your life.*

### 1. Saying No Makes Space for Yes

*One of the most beautiful aspects of saying no is that it creates space for saying yes. When you say no to things that drain you or don't align with your purpose, you free up time, energy, and resources for the things that truly matter. Suddenly, you have more space for your passions, for personal growth, for the relationships that nourish you, and for self-care.*

*Imagine this: If you say yes to every invitation, request, and commitment that comes your way, you'll eventually fill your life with obligations, leaving little room for the things that actually bring you joy. But when you practice saying no, you consciously make space for what truly lights you up. You can say yes to your dreams, yes to your creative projects, yes to your well-being.*

*Every "no" is a deliberate choice to focus your energy on what adds value to your life.*

## 2. No Means More Time for Yourself

*In a world that constantly demands our attention, saying no is a radical act of self-preservation. It allows you to take back your time, which is one of the most precious resources you have. Think about it—time is the one thing you can never get back. Once it's gone, it's gone. Saying no helps you protect that time and make it your own.*

*When you say no to unnecessary obligations, you give yourself the gift of time—time to relax, time to explore your hobbies, time to rest, and time to connect with the things and people that truly matter to you. The beauty of saying no is that it's not just about rejecting others—it's about saying yes to your own needs and desires.*

*Self-care isn't just about bubble baths and massages. It's about having the time and energy to show up for yourself, to rest, to reflect, and to create a life that feels authentic to you. Saying no is one of the most powerful tools in your self-care toolbox.*

## 3. No Helps You Build Authentic Relationships

*The fear of saying no often stems from the belief that we'll disappoint or hurt others, but the truth is, saying no can actually improve your relationships. When you set clear boundaries and say no, you teach people how to respect you and your needs. This fosters healthier, more authentic connections.*

*Imagine how exhausting it must be to say yes to everything, only to feel resentful or overextended. Those feelings can erode relationships and create tension. But when you say no, you're being honest and authentic with the people around you. You're showing them that you value yourself enough to prioritize your well-being.*

*Healthy relationships are based on mutual respect, and that includes respecting each other's time and energy. When you say no in a kind and respectful way, you create a space for more honest, meaningful connections.*

## 4. Saying No is a Form of Self-Respect

*At its core, saying no is about self-respect. It's a declaration that you value your time, your energy, and your mental well-being. It's an acknowledgment that you are worthy of putting yourself first, and that you don't need to apologize for it.*

*Think of it this way: every time you say yes to something that doesn't serve you, you're saying no to your own well-being. You're telling yourself that others' needs are more important than your own. But when you say no, you're asserting your worth and affirming that you have the right to protect your space and time.*

*Self-respect is essential to living a balanced and fulfilled life. Saying no is one of the most powerful ways to build and maintain that respect.*

## 5. The Freedom to Be Yourself

*When you start saying no, you free yourself from the constraints of others' expectations. You stop living your life based on what others think you should be doing, and instead, you create a life that is aligned with your true self. You can stop pretending to be someone you're not, stop trying to meet unrealistic standards, and stop saying yes out of obligation or fear.*

*Saying no gives you the freedom to express yourself fully, without compromise. You no longer need to please others, fit into molds, or apologize for prioritizing yourself. You can simply be who you are, live how you want to live, and enjoy the peace that comes with it.*

*In a world that constantly pulls us in different directions, saying no is a powerful act of rebellion. It's a rebellion against societal pressures, against people-pleasing, and against living a life that doesn't truly reflect who you are.*

## 6. Letting Go of the Need for Validation

*One of the most liberating aspects of saying no is the realization that you don't need external validation to feel worthy. You don't need to be constantly accepted, liked, or approved by others. When you say no, you're standing in your own power, free from the need to seek approval from anyone but yourself.*

*This shift in mindset is incredibly freeing. It allows you to make decisions based on what feels right for you, rather than based on what others might think or expect. You start to trust your own judgment, embrace your uniqueness, and live life on your own terms.*

*The more you say no to the things that don't serve you, the more you affirm that your needs, desires, and boundaries are valid—no matter what anyone else thinks..*

## 8. Saying No and Still Being a Good Person

*One of the biggest concerns people have when they start saying no is the fear that they'll be seen as selfish, rude, or uncaring. The truth is, saying no doesn't make you a bad person—it makes you a person who knows how to prioritize and respect themselves. This section will show you that it's entirely possible to say no and still be a kind, compassionate, and good person.*

## 1. The Guilt Trap

*The guilt we feel when we say no is often disproportionate to the actual impact of our decision. Many people have been taught that saying no is selfish or inconsiderate, which creates an internal conflict.*

*The fear of letting others down can be so overwhelming that we often say yes, even when we don't want to.*

*But here's the truth: guilt is a reaction, not a fact. When you say no, it's natural to feel guilty at first, but that doesn't mean you're being a bad person. Feeling guilty is just your mind trying to hold on to old patterns of behavior, where you've been conditioned to believe that saying yes is the only way to be liked or valued.*

*The more you practice saying no, the less guilty you will feel. Over time, you'll start to realize that guilt isn't a reliable indicator of your moral character—it's just an emotional response to breaking a habit. And just because someone else is disappointed by your no, doesn't mean you're wrong for saying it.*

## 2. Setting Boundaries Is an Act of Compassion

*Boundaries are essential to healthy relationships, and saying no is a key part of setting them. When you say no, you're taking care of your own needs, which is not selfish—it's necessary for your well-being. Without boundaries, we become overwhelmed, burned out, and resentful. But when we set clear limits, we can show up more fully for others, without compromising ourselves.*

*Setting boundaries also allows you to be a more honest and authentic person. When you say yes to something that you don't want to do, you're not being true to yourself, and that can lead to frustration, confusion, and even resentment. By saying no, you're being honest, which is the most compassionate thing you can do for both yourself and others.*

*Moreover, when you respect your own boundaries, you teach others how to respect them as well. You show that it's okay to say no, that it's okay to have limits, and that taking care of yourself is a priority. By modeling this behavior, you inspire others to do the same, creating a ripple effect of self-respect and healthy boundaries.*

## 3. No Does Not Mean Neglect

*Saying no doesn't mean you don't care about the person or situation—it means you care enough to protect your energy, your time, and your mental health. It's not about ignoring people or abandoning responsibilities; it's about making conscious choices that serve your greater good.*

*For example, if a friend asks for your help, but you're already overwhelmed with your own commitments, saying no doesn't mean you don't care about them. It means you care enough to be honest about your limitations. By saying no, you give yourself the opportunity to recharge, so that when you do say yes, you can give your full attention and energy to the people who need you.*

*Additionally, when you say no to something, you open up the opportunity to say yes to something that's truly aligned with your values. This allows you to invest in the things that matter most to you, and to show up in a more meaningful and impactful way.*

## 4. A Kind No Is Better Than a Hesitant Yes

*One of the biggest misconceptions about saying no is that it has to be harsh or blunt. A no doesn't have to be cold or dismissive—it can be delivered in a kind and respectful manner. In fact, saying no with kindness is often more effective and well-received than saying yes when you're not fully committed.*

*A simple, compassionate no could be something like, "I really appreciate you thinking of me, but I won't be able to take this on right now." Or, "I'd love to, but I need to take care of myself first." You don't have to justify your decision or over-explain yourself. A kind no is enough.*

*Being honest and clear with others, while still being respectful, fosters understanding and mutual respect. People will often respect your decision more when they see that you're being genuine and kind, rather than agreeing out of obligation and then being resentful.*

## 5. Saying No Saves You for the People Who Matter

*By saying no to some things, you're actually saying yes to the people and experiences that truly matter to you. If you're constantly saying yes to everything, you'll find that you have nothing left to give when it comes to the people who truly need you. But when you say no to the things that drain you, you create space for the things that nourish you.*

*This is particularly important in relationships. Saying no to things that don't align with your values or priorities allows you to show up more fully in the relationships that do matter. You can be more present, more supportive, and more loving when you have the time and energy to invest.*

*Moreover, saying no can help you avoid the trap of overcommitting. When you say yes to everything, you often end up overburdened, and your relationships suffer as a result. By setting boundaries and saying no, you give yourself the space to nurture the connections that bring you joy and fulfillment.*

## 6. Self-Care Is Not Selfish

*One of the most important lessons that comes with saying no is that self-care is not selfish. It's necessary. Taking care of your own needs is a crucial part of maintaining your mental and emotional health. When you don't make time for self-care, you risk burning out, becoming resentful, and losing sight of your own needs.*

*Saying no is a form of self-care. It's about prioritizing your own well-being and ensuring that you have the energy and capacity to give your best to others. By protecting your time and energy, you're not only taking care of yourself—you're also creating the capacity to be more present and supportive for the people who matter most in your life.*

### Conclusion: Saying No With Integrity

*Saying no is one of the most powerful tools you have in your life. It's a tool that allows you to prioritize your own well-being, protect your time, and create the life you truly want. Saying no doesn't make you a bad person; in fact, it can make you a better person by allowing you to show up in a way that is authentic, grounded, and true to who you are.*

*As you practice saying no with kindness, respect, and integrity, you'll find that it becomes easier over time. You'll start to create the life you've always wanted—one that is filled with purpose, peace, and the freedom to be yourself.*

## CHAPTER EIGHT

# CALM ON PURPOSE

*By now, you've read a few chapters.*
*You know how I write — clean, real, direct.*
*But I know what some of you might be thinking:*

*"This book's called The Philosophy of Not Giving a Damn, but it's not that dark... it's not that angry... it's not cursing every second word..."*

*Yeah.*
*And that's on purpose.*

*See, I didn't write this book to sound like a demon trapped in a hoodie.*
*I didn't write it to make people think I'm broken or bitter or bleeding rage through my pen.*
*I wrote this for clarity. For calm. For control.*
*This isn't a scream — it's a guide.*

*But don't get it twisted.*

*Just because I'm not dropping F-bombs every second sentence doesn't mean I can't.*
*Just because I'm keeping it simple doesn't mean I'm not capable of writing the darkest, most brutal, most emotionally violent shit you've ever read.*

*Wanna see what I mean?*

*? Exhibit A — The Rage Version:*

*"You're stuck in a cycle of giving a fuck about people who wouldn't lift a finger if you were hanging off the edge of your sanity. You break your back for their comfort. You sell your soul for their approval. Fuck that. Stop begging. Stop explaining. Start disappearing."*

*? Exhibit B — The War Mode Version:*

*"The world doesn't give a single fuck if you drown, as long as you smile while you're sinking. So sink with a smile? Hell no. Burn the water. Cut the ropes. Save yourself. Let them choke on the silence you leave behind."*

*Yeah. I could've written the whole damn book like that.*
*Each page dripping in anger and fire.*
*Each line punching teeth instead of patting backs.*
*That kind of writing? It hits — but it also drags you into a certain place.*
*And I didn't write this to drag you down.*


*I wrote it to lift you the fuck out.*


*This book is for people who are exhausted.*
*Not bitter — just tired.*
*Not evil — just done.*
*Done with fake smiles.*
*Done with chasing approval.*
*Done with constantly explaining themselves to people who don't even try to understand.*


*That's who I'm writing for.*


*I didn't choose clean, sharp, clear language because I'm soft.*
*I chose it because you're already drowning in noise.*
*You don't need more rage.*
*You need release.*


*And yeah — some of you may crave the savage tone.*
*You want every chapter to slap.*
*You want lines like:*

*"If they don't love you at your worst, leave them the fuck there. You're not a rehab center for emotionally dead humans."*

*Or:*

*"You're not Jesus — stop dying for people who wouldn't even text you back if you went missing."*

*And I feel that.*
*Sometimes you need fire.*
*But sometimes, what you need more... is silence.*
*Sometimes the most powerful thing isn't shouting,*
*it's finally walking away without saying a word.*

*So yeah, I can write like that.*
*But I won't — not for this book.*

*Because this isn't about being edgy.*
*This isn't about being "cool angry."*
*This is about being peaceful as fuck in a world that*
*wants your energy bleeding out 24/7.*

*So next time you think,*
*"Damn, this could've gone darker..."*

*Just know:*
*It could have.*
*But I didn't let it.*
*Because I'm not writing to be feared.*
*I'm writing to remind you:*
*You can let go...*
*And still be a savage in silence.*


*Back to the mission.*

## CHAPTER NINE

# THE BURDEN OF EXPECTATIONS

## 1. The Inherited Script

*From the very moment we're born, we're handed an invisible script—an outline for how we should live, what we should pursue, and who we should become. This script is rarely one that we've written ourselves. It's crafted by the world around us—by our family, our culture, our society, and even by strangers who never really know us. These expectations are stitched into the fabric of our lives, and before we even have a chance to understand who we are, we are already told how to behave, what to strive for, and what success should look like.*

*Think about it for a moment. What was the first expectation you can remember being placed upon you? Was it the pressure to get good grades? To be polite and well-behaved? To pursue a particular career or follow a specific path because that's what was expected of you? As children, we begin to internalize these rules without even questioning them. Our parents tell us what's right or wrong, our teachers give us a set of goals to reach, and society sends us constant messages about what it means to be "successful."*

*But here's the critical question we rarely ask ourselves—**who wrote this script?** Who decided what success looks like? Who decided that we should be married by a certain age, that we should have a high-paying job, or that we should prioritize others' needs over our own? These expectations often come from well-meaning people in our lives, but the truth is, they don't always reflect our true desires, values, or goals.*

*As we grow, the inherited script becomes more ingrained. We start to live according to what others expect from us instead of questioning whether these expectations align with our own hearts. We fall into a cycle of trying to meet the standards that others set—whether it's pursuing a particular career, achieving a level of success that's been defined for us, or even living up to physical or social expectations. In the process, we often lose touch with who we are and what we really want. The script may be written in good faith, but it doesn't account for the nuances of our unique experiences and identities.*

*One of the most powerful realizations we can have in life is recognizing that we **have the power to rewrite our script.** The truth is that there is no single,* universal path that we must follow. Success is subjective, happiness is personal, and fulfillment doesn't look the same for everyone. The very idea of success, for instance, is a deeply personal thing. For some, success may look like climbing the corporate ladder, while for others, it could mean building a small business or living a minimalist lifestyle. The challenge is to **question the default script** that has been handed to us and ask ourselves: **What does success mean to me? What does fulfillment look like in my life?**

For example, think about a common script many of us are given: the path of education, career, and marriage. From a young age, we are told that we should go to school, get good grades, go to college, and land a high-paying job. Then, after achieving this, the next expected milestone is to settle down, get married, and start a family. These expectations are often so deeply ingrained that we might never think to question them until we find ourselves living a life that feels like it's not our own.

The trouble with following this script is that it doesn't account for individual desires or personal growth. It's one-size-fits-all, and not everyone fits into the same mold. What if you don't want to follow this typical trajectory? What if you want to travel the world, pursue a passion that doesn't lead to a high-paying job, or live a life that doesn't revolve around traditional family structures? The challenge is recognizing that you are not bound by the script. **You can break free from it**—but first, you must be aware of it. And then, you must have the courage to ask,

*"What do I truly want?" instead of "What is expected of me?"*

*The moment we begin to question the inherited script, we open ourselves up to a world of possibilities. We can begin to shape our own narrative. It's like being handed a blank page and realizing that the story doesn't have to follow the one that's been written for us. We have the pen in our hands. But the question remains—**will we dare to rewrite the story?***

*Rewriting your own script doesn't mean you have to rebel against all societal expectations or abandon everything that others have recommended for you. It's about understanding that **you have the right to make your own decisions**—decisions that are grounded in your own values, desires, and vision for the future. When you take the time to pause and reflect on your life, you begin to realize that the answers you've been searching for are already within you. You don't need permission from anyone else to live your life in a way that feels authentic to you.*

## 2. The Silent Pressure

*Expectations aren't always loud or overt. In fact, the most powerful and insidious ones often come in the form of **silent pressure**—the subtle, unspoken forces that push us in directions we didn't necessarily choose for ourselves. These pressures aren't always articulated directly, but they shape our behaviors,* *decisions, and even our self-perception. We're constantly absorbing signals from the world around us—through social media, the stories of others, or the subtle cues we pick up in our interactions with family, friends, and colleagues. And because they're so quiet, we often don't recognize how much they're influencing us until we stop and really think about it.*

*The silent pressure can take on many forms. One of the most common is the **pressure to conform**—the implicit understanding that if you're different or don't fit into the norm, you might be judged, excluded, or misunderstood. Whether it's the pressure to dress a certain way, act a certain way, or even talk a certain way, we're constantly being nudged to fit into a specific mold. When we deviate from this mold, we might feel like we're walking on thin ice, constantly trying to avoid the gaze of others who might deem us "weird" or "unusual."*

*We see this pressure play out in everyday scenarios. Take social media, for example. Platforms are designed to reward conformity—whether it's presenting a curated version of your life, sharing moments that fit into a predefined narrative of success, or showcasing a lifestyle that others might aspire to. The constant flow of idealized images and lifestyles can create an underlying feeling that if we don't measure up, we're somehow failing. But the truth is, social media rarely shows the full picture. It's easy to get caught in a cycle of comparison, believing that the carefully crafted version of someone else's life is the standard we should live by.*

*Then there's the **pressure to be liked**. From a young age, we're taught the importance of being "social" and "liked." Whether it's trying to make friends in school, gaining approval from family, or fitting in with a peer group, the desire to be accepted is a natural human impulse. But this desire can sometimes evolve into something unhealthy—when we begin to mold ourselves into what others want us to be, rather than staying true to who we are. We start making decisions based on the fear of rejection rather than the pursuit of our own happiness. We do things, say things, or act in ways that will please others, even if it means compromising our own values.*

*The pressure to fit in is something that can haunt us well into adulthood. At work, we feel the need to meet the expectations of our boss or colleagues—working harder, saying yes to more tasks, and pushing ourselves past our limits just to prove that we're capable and worthy of recognition. In relationships, we might feel the pressure to live up to an ideal of what a partner, friend, or family member should be. We adjust ourselves to meet others' expectations, often losing sight of who we are in the process. And even in seemingly small, everyday moments, we feel the weight of social norms—the expectations about how we should speak, how we should look, or how we should behave in public.*

*But the most dangerous part of all this silent pressure is that it's not always easy to recognize. It's often* **hidden beneath layers of well-meaning advice**, *societal norms, and a desire to "fit in." It can be so ingrained that it becomes our default setting, operating in the background of our lives without our full awareness. We may go through life feeling like we're not measuring up, but we often don't pause to ask ourselves, "Is this really my expectation or someone else's?"*

*As we grow older, we may find ourselves questioning why we're unhappy or unfulfilled, despite meeting all the milestones society has set out for us. We might have the career, the relationship, the possessions, the status—but still feel a deep sense of emptiness. This is because we've been living in response to external pressures, not internal desires. The problem with* **living according to others' expectations** *is that it creates a sense of* **disconnection from our authentic selves.** *We're so focused on meeting the demands placed upon us that we forget to check in with our own needs, dreams, and aspirations.*

*The weight of this silent pressure is not something we always feel consciously. It's a slow build-up—a series of small compromises over time that add up to a significant loss of identity. We may start out with a clear sense of who we are, but slowly, the influence of societal expectations erodes our true self. We find ourselves waking up one day and asking, "Who am I really? What do I truly want from life?" And it's only at that point that we realize how much of our lives have been shaped by external forces, and how little we've truly followed our own internal compass.*

*It's not easy to break free from this silent pressure, because it's so deeply embedded in our culture and daily lives. But the first step is* **awareness.** *We need to recognize when we're living in response to external pressures rather than authentic desires. It starts with being honest with ourselves about why we're making the choices we are. Are we doing this because it aligns with our values, or are we doing it because we're* *afraid of being judged, left out, or unappreciated? The more we tune into our true feelings and needs, the easier it becomes to distinguish between what is truly our own choice and what is simply an attempt to fit into someone else's mold.*

*As we begin to strip away these layers of external pressure, we start to experience a sense of freedom. We begin to realize that we don't have to conform to anyone else's idea of success or happiness. We can define those things for ourselves. The more we reject the silent pressures of society, the more we free ourselves to live a life that's* **authentically ours**—*one that reflects our own values, desires, and vision for the future.*

### 3. The Cost of Compliance

*Living in compliance with the expectations of others comes at a steep cost—often, one we don't realize until it's too late. Every time we suppress our true desires, our individuality, and our authentic selves to meet the demands of others, we pay a price. The cost can be seen in our* **mental health, emotional well-being**, *and* **overall happiness***.*

*At first, compliance might feel like the right choice. After all, we want to be accepted. We want to feel like we belong. We want to make our parents, our friends, or our society proud. And so, we comply—consciously or unconsciously—by following the path set out for us by others. But the longer we stay on this path, the more disconnected we become from our own identity.* **We stop asking, "What do I want?" and start asking, "What do they expect?"** *And in this shift, we lose ourselves.*

*The true cost of compliance is a* **loss of self.** *As we live according to the expectations of others, we start to forget who we are beneath the roles we play. We start to believe that* **our worth is determined by external factors**—*our achievements, our social status, and the approval of others—rather than by who we truly are at our core. Over time, this disconnect erodes our sense of self-worth and leaves us feeling unfulfilled, lost, and disconnected from our true passions.*

*One of the most insidious consequences of compliance is* **burnout.** *When we are constantly chasing the approval of others, we push ourselves beyond our limits, trying to meet expectations that were never ours to begin with. We sacrifice our time, energy, and emotional well-being to fulfill others' needs, often leaving little to no room for ourselves. Eventually, this leads to exhaustion, resentment, and frustration. The result?* **A deep sense of emptiness** *that no amount of external validation can fill.*

*This emptiness can manifest in many forms:* **anxiety, depression, confusion, and self-doubt.** *We look at the life we've built—the job we've taken, the relationships we've fostered, the decisions we've made—and wonder how we got here. We question* *whether it's truly our life or if we've been living someone else's dream.*

*Furthermore, the constant pressure to comply also **limits our potential.** When we live to meet the expectations of others, we often hold ourselves back from pursuing our true passions. We bury our dreams, telling ourselves they are unrealistic or impractical. We stop taking risks, afraid of disappointing those around us. But the truth is, **the biggest risk we can take is to never take any risks at all.** By staying in compliance with others' expectations, we stay stuck in a life that isn't ours—preventing us from ever truly living to our fullest potential.*

*Ultimately, **the cost of compliance is the loss of our authenticity,** and the consequences of losing our authenticity are far more damaging than the discomfort of breaking free. Compliance is a slow death of the soul, and we must ask ourselves: **Is living someone else's life really worth the price?***

## 4. Breaking Free

*Breaking free from the expectations of others is not an easy task—it's a journey of rediscovery, courage, and self-love. It involves **taking a step back** from the life you've built and asking yourself, "Is this really what I want?" And when the answer is no, it's about having the strength to walk away from everything that no longer serves you.*

*The first step in breaking free is **becoming aware of the expectations you've been living under.** These expectations might be so deeply ingrained that you don't even realize they're there. They could be expectations from your parents, your friends, your community, or even from yourself. Perhaps you've always been told that success looks a certain way, that you need to follow a certain path, or that you must conform to societal standards. The key here is to **acknowledge these expectations** for what they are—not truths, but imposed beliefs that don't necessarily reflect who you are or what you desire.*

*Once you've recognized the expectations you've been living by, the next step is to **question them.** Do these expectations align with your true values? Are they helping you grow, or are they keeping you stuck? Start asking yourself whether the choices you've been making are truly your own. Are you pursuing a career, relationship, or lifestyle because you genuinely want to, or are you doing it to satisfy the needs of others? **It's time to challenge these beliefs and ask whether they are serving your highest good.***

*Breaking free also means **learning to disappoint others**—and understanding that this is not a reflection of your worth. The fear of disappointing others is a huge barrier for many people when it comes to living authentically. We worry that if we stop meeting others' expectations, they will reject us or no longer love us. But the truth is, **people who truly care about you will respect your choices**, even if they don't always understand them. And if someone's love or approval is contingent upon your compliance with their expectations, then perhaps that relationship needs to be reexamined.*

*At this point, the journey requires **courage and commitment**. Breaking free is about stepping into the unknown. It's about embracing the uncertainty that comes with forging your own path and trusting that you are capable of creating a life that aligns with your true self. It may be uncomfortable at first—change always is—but it's important to remind yourself that discomfort is a natural part of growth. **Nothing great comes from staying in your comfort zone.***

*As you begin to break free, **you will also have to embrace your imperfections**. There is no "perfect" way to live authentically. Your choices may not always be perfect, and there will be mistakes along the way. But that's okay. What matters is that you are living in a way that feels true to who you are, and you're not afraid to course-correct when necessary. The journey is not linear, and there will be challenges—but these challenges are part of what makes it worthwhile.*

*One of the most powerful steps in breaking free is **taking ownership of your life.** When you stop living for others and start living for yourself, you reclaim your personal power. This is not about being selfish or reckless; it's about making the conscious decision to **put yourself first.** When you prioritize your own happiness, well-being, and dreams, you create the space to live a more fulfilling, meaningful life.*

***Breaking free is a declaration of self-worth.** It's a commitment to honoring your truth, even when it's hard, even when it requires sacrifice. It's about giving yourself permission to be yourself, without apology or compromise. And in this journey, you will begin to experience the incredible freedom that comes from being true to who you are—not who others expect you to be.*

**5. *Living on Your Own Terms***

*The true meaning of freedom lies in being able to live life according to your own terms. Too often, we find ourselves in a constant struggle between **who we are** and **who we think we should be**. The pressure to meet the expectations of others can distort our sense of self and cause us to chase goals that aren't ours. But real freedom isn't just about getting rid of external pressures; it's about **reclaiming control over your own life**, setting your own boundaries, and choosing what matters most to you, regardless of what anyone else thinks or expects.*

*Living on your own terms doesn't mean being reckless or selfish—it means honoring your own desires, values, and needs above all else. It's about deciding that you are worthy of a life that aligns with who you truly are, not who others want you to be. The journey toward this kind of freedom begins when we stop seeking approval from external sources and start looking inward, to discover what truly brings us joy, fulfillment, and peace.*

*In our journey of self-discovery, we must first accept that **we don't owe anyone an explanation for living authentically.** The idea that we must constantly justify our choices to others is a remnant of societal conditioning. Whether it's our career choices, our relationships, or the way we live our day-to-day lives, we often feel obligated to explain ourselves or gain the approval of others. But the reality is, **we are the only ones who truly understand the reasons behind our decisions.** And those reasons need to be rooted in our own truth, not in the expectations of others.*

*To live on your own terms, you must first **redefine success.** Too often, we measure our success against a standard set by society—graduating from a prestigious university, landing a high-paying job, owning a big house, and accumulating material wealth. While these things can bring comfort, they don't necessarily bring fulfillment. True success isn't about meeting society's benchmarks; it's about achieving a life that feels meaningful and true to your values. For some, this might mean pursuing a creative passion, traveling the world, or choosing a career that brings joy instead of status. Success is about finding your own path, regardless of whether it aligns with mainstream ideas of what's "successful."*

***Setting your own boundaries** is another crucial aspect of living on your own terms. Boundaries are not just about saying "no" to others—they're about saying "yes" to yourself. They are the invisible lines you draw in your life to protect your time, energy, and emotional well-being. When you live with clear* *boundaries, you take responsibility for your happiness and stop allowing others to dictate your choices. Whether it's turning down a job offer that doesn't align with your values or choosing to walk away from a relationship that no longer serves you, setting boundaries allows you to create space for the things that matter most to you.*

*As you begin to live on your own terms, you will inevitably encounter resistance.* **People will not always understand** *your choices, and that's okay. In fact, it's often a sign that you're moving in the right direction. When you decide to break free from the expectations of others, you are challenging the status quo, and that can make some people uncomfortable. But you don't have to apologize for choosing yourself.* **Your happiness, peace, and well-being are not negotiable.** *And while it's important to consider the feelings of those you care about, you are not responsible for their reactions to your choices. They, too, must take responsibility for their own lives, just as you are taking responsibility for yours.*

*Living on your own terms is a radical act of self-love and self-respect. It's a decision to value yourself enough to create the life you truly want.* **It's about knowing that you are deserving of a life filled with joy, fulfillment, and peace—and that this life can only be created when you stop living for the approval of others.** *This means embracing your own individuality and letting go of the need for external validation. When you do this, you free yourself from the prison of other people's expectations and step into* *your true power.*

*Trusting yourself is the cornerstone of this journey. When you stop relying on the opinions of others and start trusting your own instincts, you unlock a whole new level of confidence. You no longer have to second-guess your choices or seek constant reassurance. Instead, you move forward with the certainty that your path is the right one for you. It may not always be easy, and there will be times when doubt creeps in, but when you have faith in your own judgment, you'll always be able to find your way back to yourself.*

*Living on your own terms also involves a willingness to embrace the unknown. We often resist change because it's uncomfortable. The familiar, even if it's unhealthy or unfulfilling, feels safe. But true growth only happens when we step outside our comfort zones. The journey to living authentically is a leap into the unknown, and with every step, you will discover new things about yourself that you never knew existed. It's about trusting that the universe will support you as you carve out your own path, even if that path looks different from what anyone else expects.*

*Living on your own terms is not a one-time decision—it's a daily practice. It's a commitment to staying true to yourself every single day, regardless of external pressure. Some days will be harder than others, but with each day that you live authentically, you build resilience and inner strength. You teach yourself that you are enough, just as you are, and that you don't have to conform to anyone else's idea of what you should be. Over time, this practice becomes a habit, and the more you live on your own terms, the more you will experience a deep sense of peace, contentment, and fulfillment.*

*So, stop measuring yourself against the standards set by others. Stop seeking approval. Stop living in the shadows of other people's dreams.* **It's time to start living for yourself,** *to embrace who you truly are, and to create a life that reflects your deepest desires. When you do this, you will experience the freedom that comes with knowing that your life is uniquely yours—and that it's up to you, and only you, to determine what that life looks like.*

*As you stand at the crossroads of your life, remember that* **the greatest act of courage** *is not in conforming to the expectations of others, but in* **choosing to live as you are, unapologetically and authentically.** *The world may try to define you, but only you hold the power to write your own story.*

*In the quiet moments when you feel the weight of others' desires pulling at your soul, pause, breathe, and ask yourself:* **Is this my path? Is this my truth?** *If the answer is no, then it's time to take the first step towards your own freedom—***the freedom to be yourself, to love yourself, and to live a life that's truly yours.**

*Don't be afraid to walk away from what no longer serves you. The path ahead may be uncertain, but it is yours to create. And with each step you take, you will find that the life you've been seeking was always within you, waiting to be unlocked.*

*So let go. Walk away from the expectations. Walk toward the life you deserve—one built on your terms, your values, and your dreams.*

*The world is full of endless possibilities, and the moment you choose yourself, you will begin to see them unfold.*

"The true freedom lies not in the absence of chains, but in the courage to break them and walk your own path."

## CHAPTER TEN

# THE ART OF WALKING AWAY

## 1. The Power of Letting Go

*Letting go is a transformative act, a declaration that you are no longer willing to stay in situations that drain your energy or limit your potential. It goes beyond simply **leaving** a place or person; it's about emotionally releasing the **weight** that keeps you tethered to things that no longer serve you. The real power of letting go comes from knowing **when to stop fighting battles that aren't yours to win** and instead focus on creating a future that feels aligned with your values, desires, and purpose.*

*Letting go is a process that can feel **unnatural** at first. Society has ingrained in us that we should be **committed**—to relationships, jobs, or social expectations. We often feel guilty about leaving something behind, fearing judgment or disapproval from others. But in truth, letting go is a **form of*** *self-care*, even if it's uncomfortable. It's an essential practice that helps you clear emotional clutter and make room for new possibilities.

The art of walking away is a form of **emotional intelligence**. It's the ability to assess your situation, listen to your inner voice, and realize that sometimes you must walk away to preserve your mental health, your peace of mind, and ultimately, your happiness. **Freedom** comes from detaching from what's not working—whether it's a negative thought pattern, a toxic relationship, or a job that makes you feel small.

For instance, I've personally walked away from friendships that were once meaningful. These friendships turned out to be emotionally draining, where I constantly felt like I was the one putting in effort, and the return was minimal. The decision to step away wasn't easy, but it was necessary. It felt like I was shedding **old skin**, making space for healthier connections and a clearer sense of self. The truth is, we don't have the emotional capacity to hold onto everything. **Sometimes, holding on to everything keeps us from holding on to what truly matters.**

*Letting go might not come naturally, and at times it might feel like an act of surrender. But surrendering isn't weakness; it's* **strength**. *It's recognizing that you are powerful enough to move on from things that do not serve your highest good. And in this decision, you* **empower yourself** *to grow in new, uncharted directions.*

## 2. Signs It's Time to Walk Away

*Walking away is not a decision that should be made lightly, but there are signs that will guide you toward realizing that it might be time to make the change. In the beginning, these signs might be subtle—an uneasy feeling in the pit of your stomach, or a nagging thought that won't go away. But as you pay closer attention, they'll become clearer, and eventually, undeniable.*

- **You constantly feel drained, anxious, or unfulfilled.**

*Emotional exhaustion can sneak up on you. You may be going through the motions, trying to maintain your daily routines, but deep down, you know something isn't right. If you constantly feel tired, even after a good night's sleep, or if your energy is constantly depleted by certain people or situations, it's time to pay attention to those cues.* **Emotional burnout** *happens when we give so much of ourselves to others or to a situation that we forget to nourish ourselves. Over time, it leaves you feeling empty, anxious, and unfulfilled.*

*Imagine working at a job that no longer challenges or excites you. Every morning, you drag yourself out of bed, not because you're eager to contribute or create, but because you're doing it out of **habit**. That's not living. That's simply surviving. When you feel like your job, relationships, or daily life is **sapping** your energy without replenishing it, the act of walking away becomes a form of self-preservation.*

- **Your presence is tolerated, not valued.**

*Being **tolerated** can be one of the most disheartening experiences. It can feel like you're invisible, like no one sees you for who you truly are. It's an experience that many of us encounter in toxic work environments or in relationships where we are seen as a "**necessary nuisance**" rather than a valued contributor.*

***Example:*** *Think about a work environment where your input is often ignored or dismissed, and you feel like an afterthought. Or a friendship where you've always been the one reaching out, and no one ever reciprocates. Eventually, you start feeling like you're more of an **accessory** than a participant. This feeling* is a sign. **You deserve to be in places and relationships where you feel appreciated, heard, and seen.** And if you aren't, it may be time to walk away.


- 
  **You're staying out of guilt, fear, or obligation—not desire.**


One of the biggest obstacles to walking away is guilt. Guilt can keep you tied to situations that don't serve you, simply because you fear disappointing someone else. Fear of being labeled as selfish, ungrateful, or disloyal can hold us in situations much longer than we should be. The truth is, staying out of guilt is **counterproductive.** You can't be fully present for others if you're not taking care of yourself first.


**Take for instance a family situation**—maybe you feel guilty about distancing yourself from a relative who has been emotionally abusive. Or perhaps you're staying in a friendship because the other person needs you, even though it feels draining. Guilt keeps us stuck. Walking away doesn't mean abandoning others; it means choosing to honor your own **boundaries** and **mental health.**


- 
  **You feel like you're betraying yourself by staying.**

*Sometimes, when we stay in situations that no longer serve us, we begin to feel as though we are betraying the **core of who we are**. You might feel that your values, beliefs, and goals no longer align with what you are staying in. You might even feel like you've lost your sense of self. This is a wake-up call. When your presence in a relationship or a job starts feeling like a betrayal of your true self, it's time to walk away.*

**Example:** *A person who has been in a long-term relationship may feel that they've outgrown it, that their needs have changed. If they continue staying out of obligation, they may end up resenting both their partner and themselves. The moment you feel **disconnected** from your authentic self, that's a sign that change is necessary.*

- **Growth is impossible in the current situation.**

**Growth** *is an essential part of life. If you are no longer growing or evolving in a particular environment, it's like trying to fill a cup that's already full. In relationships, careers, or even friendships, you should feel challenged in healthy ways. If that challenge doesn't exist anymore, staying becomes **unproductive**. The environment you're in becomes stagnant, and without growth, life can become **mundane**.*

*It's like outgrowing a pair of shoes. At one point, they fit perfectly, but now, they are too tight. Staying in them only causes discomfort. Sometimes, to continue growing, you have to **let go of what no longer fits**.*

### 3. Overcoming the Fear of Leaving

*Fear is the number one thing that keeps people from taking that leap to walk away. The fear of **what's next**, the fear of **disappointing others**, and the fear of **failure**. But here's the thing: Fear, if left unchecked, will keep you stuck in situations that make you unhappy, **draining the life out of you. Fear of change** is normal, but it shouldn't control you.*

***Example:** You might have a job that's comfortable but unfulfilling. You might be terrified of the unknown if you leave, not knowing how you'll financially survive or if you'll find a new opportunity. But fear of the unknown is just that—**fear**. There are no guarantees in life, but there are opportunities. And if you stay in a situation simply because you're afraid to leave, you're choosing **stagnation** over **growth**.*

*To break through this fear, shift your mindset:*

- *
    **Shift your perspective:** Focus on the **freedom** that will come with leaving. Ask yourself, "What do I*

*stand to gain?" and shift away from the fear of loss.*

- ***Embrace discomfort:*** *Walking away from something familiar is uncomfortable, but **staying stuck is more uncomfortable** in the long run.*

- ***Reaffirm your decision:*** *Remind yourself why you're leaving. Write it down and keep it visible to reinforce your decision whenever doubt sneaks in.*

## 4. Walking Away Without Guilt & Moving Forward

One of the hardest challenges in the process of walking away is releasing the **guilt** that often follows. Guilt is a powerful emotion that can creep in quietly, making you second-guess your decisions and causing you to feel like you've done something wrong. You may feel like you're betraying someone, disappointing them, or abandoning them when you choose to walk away from a relationship, a job, or a situation that has become toxic or draining. But let me remind you of this simple truth: **You are not responsible for someone else's happiness**, nor should your life be dictated by the comfort of others at the expense of your own well-being.

It's easy to convince yourself that you should stay in a situation for the sake of others. Maybe you've stayed in a friendship because you didn't want to hurt *someone's feelings. Or you've kept a toxic job because you feared the consequences of quitting, even though every day it takes a toll on your mental and physical health. But staying out of guilt doesn't help anyone.* **It perpetuates a cycle of resentment, self-neglect, and unhappiness.** *When you allow guilt to control your decisions, you're telling yourself that your own happiness, health, and growth are less important than someone else's comfort.*

*Letting go of this guilt involves* **reaffirming your worth** *and recognizing that prioritizing yourself is not selfish—it's essential. Here's how you can walk away with confidence and release guilt along the way:*

- **Recognize the importance of self-care:** *Just as you can't pour from an empty cup, you can't be the best version of yourself for others if you're not taking care of your own emotional, physical, and mental health. When you start to see walking away as a form of self-care, it becomes easier to accept that your needs matter too.*

- **Understand that people will adjust:** *One of the reasons we hold on to guilt is the fear that others won't know how to cope without us. This can be especially difficult if you're leaving behind a family member, partner, or friend who depends on you. But remember, while it might be tough for them initially, they will adapt. People are resilient, and just as you have to adjust to new circumstances,* *so can they. Disappointment is temporary, but the effects of staying in a situation that doesn't serve you are long-term.* **Their adjustment will be temporary, but your well-being is permanent.**

- **Know that you can't heal in the same environment that hurt you**: *If you stay in a toxic situation out of guilt, you're prolonging your own suffering. You can't heal if you keep subjecting yourself to the same harmful conditions. Walking away is your way of choosing health, peace, and growth, and that should never be seen as selfish. In fact, it's the* **most loving thing you can do—for yourself and others**. *By leaving, you make space for better opportunities, healthier connections, and a life that brings you true fulfillment.*

- **Own your decision**: *The more you own your decision to walk away, the less guilt will be able to hold you back. When you take full responsibility for your choices and reaffirm that they are made with your best interests in mind, the guilt begins to lose its power. Walk away with confidence, knowing that you are making the best decision for yourself. The more resolute you are, the less you'll feel the pull of guilt trying to drag you back into something that no longer serves you.*

*Moving Forward: The True Power of Walking Away*

*Once you've walked away from something that no longer serves you—whether it's a relationship, a job, or even a certain way of thinking—the next phase begins: **moving forward**. This part of the journey can be both exhilarating and challenging. You're entering into unknown territory, free from the constraints of the past, but you're also starting over in some respects. It's like planting seeds in a garden—at first, there's nothing to show for your efforts, but in time, the fruits of your labor will emerge.*

*Moving forward after walking away is not simply about leaving things behind; it's about **creating space for new growth**. It's about redefining who you are and what you truly want out of life. It's about learning from the past and using that wisdom to build a future that aligns with your authentic self.*

*Here's how you can move forward and embrace the freedom that comes with walking away:*

1.

*Give yourself time to heal*: After leaving behind something significant, it's important to take time for **reflection** and **healing**. You may feel lost, unsure, or even a little scared, but that's okay. Healing doesn't happen overnight. Give yourself permission to feel all the emotions that come with walking away—grief, relief, fear, excitement—**all of it** is part of the process. But understand that healing is a **necessary** step to becoming the best version of yourself. Don't rush through it.

2.

*Set new intentions*: Now that you've cleared the space by walking away, it's time to **set new intentions**. What do you want for your life? What kind of person do you want to become? What are your values, and how can you align your actions with them moving forward? This is a time to reconnect with your passions and desires. **Start small**, but make sure every step you take is aligned with your goals and the life you envision.

For example, after leaving a draining job, you may decide to pursue something you've always been passionate about, like starting a business or going back to school. Or, if you've walked away from a relationship, you may want to take time to focus on your **own growth** and self-love before jumping into another connection. Every decision you make can be a building block toward the life you want.

1.

***Embrace the unknown:*** *Walking away opens up new possibilities, but those possibilities are often hidden in the unknown. The fear of uncertainty can hold many people back from taking that step, but remember,* **the unknown is where all the magic happens.** *It's where you grow, where you discover new opportunities, and where you learn to trust yourself in ways you never have before. There is beauty in the journey forward, even when the path seems unclear.* **Embrace the mystery** *and let it excite you rather than scare you.*

2.

***Build a strong support system:*** *As you move forward, it's important to surround yourself with people who uplift and support you. The right people will help you grow and stay grounded, especially when doubt creeps in. Seek out relationships that bring positivity, encouragement, and understanding. If you've walked away from toxic connections, don't settle for anything less than* **genuine, healthy relationships** *moving forward. You deserve it.*

3.

*Accept that there will be setbacks: Moving forward doesn't mean the journey will be smooth. There will be bumps along the road. But setbacks are not signs that you've made the wrong decision—they are simply part of the process of growth. Sometimes, you'll feel like you're taking two steps forward and one step back.* **That's okay.** *Keep going. Every challenge is an opportunity to learn more about yourself and what you want out of life.*

In the end, walking away isn't about **giving up;** it's about **choosing yourself.** When you make the decision to leave what's no longer serving you, you make room for something better to come into your life. **The art of walking away is ultimately the art of embracing freedom,** freedom to grow, evolve, and create the life you truly want. It's about taking your power back, setting boundaries, and saying to yourself, "I deserve better." And when you learn to do this, you'll find that the future holds endless possibilities. **Your life is yours to shape—**and by walking away from what doesn't serve you, you are taking the first courageous step toward creating a life that truly fulfills you.

"In the art of walking away, we don't just leave behind what no longer serves us; we make space for the life we are yet to discover."

## CHAPTER ELEVEN

# THE CALL OF YOUR DREAM

*Every dream begins with a whisper—a soft and gentle calling that echoes through the deepest part of your being. It might be a fleeting thought, a spark of inspiration, or a sudden realization. It's that idea you can't shake, the vision you keep coming back to, no matter how far you push it away. At first, it feels almost intangible—something that exists in the realm of "maybe" or "someday." But despite its haziness, something deep within tells you that this dream is yours, that it's meant to be pursued.*

*The dream starts small—just a seed planted in the fertile soil of your mind. It might look like a simple desire: to start a business, to travel the world, to write a book, or to master a craft. But as time passes, the seed grows, and with it, the awareness that this is more than just a wish. It's a part of you. Your soul recognizes it, even if your mind hasn't fully caught up yet.*

*In the beginning, your dream feels distant—perhaps even unreachable. You might wonder if you have what it takes.* **What if you fail?** *What if others don't understand? The fear of the unknown can be paralyzing, and that fear often quiets the voice of your dream. But no matter how hard you try to ignore it, it keeps calling, pulling at your heartstrings, reminding you that* **this dream is yours and yours alone.** *It doesn't matter what anyone else thinks. What matters is that you feel it in your bones, that you can't escape it, no matter how hard you try.*

*But dreams don't stay quiet for long. The longer you ignore them, the louder they become. They don't fade into the background or disappear into thin air. Instead, they start to show up in every corner of your life—in the books you read, the movies you watch, the conversations you overhear. They sneak into your thoughts during quiet moments, and they invade your daydreams.* **Your dream begins to take root,** *and the more it grows, the more impossible it feels to walk away from.*

*There's something incredibly powerful about a dream that is meant for you.* **It doesn't belong to anyone else.** *You can't compare it to the dreams of others, nor can you measure its worth against society's standards of success. Your dream is unique—tailored to your strengths, your passions, your purpose. It's something that only you can bring into the world, and it's the life force that fuels your drive.*

*So, the real question is not whether you're capable of achieving your dream, but whether you're willing to take that first step. Dreams require action. They demand courage, persistence, and a willingness to face the unknown. But they also bring with them an unparalleled sense of fulfillment.* **The dream isn't just a goal. It's a path, a journey that will transform you.**

*And though the road may be rocky, and the destination uncertain, the journey itself is where you'll find the most growth, the most joy, and the most purpose.* **The call of your dream is not a suggestion—it's an invitation to step into the person you were always meant to be.** *It's a challenge to rise above your doubts, to push past your fears, and to take the leap toward something greater than yourself.*

*As the dream continues to call to you, your responsibility is not to wait for the perfect moment or the right conditions, but to respond.* **You don't need to know everything before you start.** *You don't need a roadmap, a plan, or a guarantee of success. What you need is the belief that this dream is worth pursuing, and the courage to step into the unknown, one step at a time.*

**So listen closely.** *The whisper is no longer faint. It's a call you can no longer ignore.* **It's time to follow it.**

## 2. The Fear of the Unknown

*The fear of the unknown is perhaps the most insidious barrier between where you are and where you want to be. It's a force that holds you captive, keeping you tethered to a life of comfort and familiarity, even when your heart craves change.* **The unknown** *is not just the physical territory you haven't yet explored, but also the emotional, mental, and spiritual spaces you've never dared to enter.*

*At its core, fear of the unknown is born from uncertainty. It's the fear of stepping into a space where there are no guarantees, no clear path, and no promises of success. It's easier to stay where things are predictable, even if they no longer serve you. The known feels safe, even if that safety comes at the cost of your dreams. It's the quiet comfort of stagnation—a place where you can numb your desires and hide from the very thing you need most: growth.*

*But here's the truth:* **Growth cannot happen in the comfort zone.** *The unknown is not a void; it's a fertile ground where transformation takes root. It's a space full of possibility, waiting for you to have the courage to step into it. The challenge is, of course, that* **we fear what we cannot control.** *We fear what we cannot predict, what we cannot see. The unknown is a giant question mark, and our instinct is to avoid anything that we can't fully grasp or understand.*

*This fear manifests in different ways. It might show up as procrastination, as self-doubt, or as the constant questioning of whether you are good enough. Sometimes, it looks like paralyzing indecision—where you know you want to make a change but feel overwhelmed by the weight of what lies ahead. The fear of the unknown can even prevent you from making small decisions, leaving you stuck in a cycle of inaction and frustration. The irony?* **Staying stuck is the greatest risk you can take.**

*So, why do we let this fear hold us back? Part of it lies in our wiring. As humans, we have an inherent need for security. Evolutionarily, we were designed to avoid risks that could lead to harm or danger. But in modern life, those primal instincts don't always serve us well. The fear of stepping into the unknown might be rooted in our survival instincts, but in the context of following our dreams, it becomes a barrier to living a fulfilled and meaningful life.*

*The truth is, the unknown isn't something to be afraid of—it's something to embrace.* **The unknown is where the magic happens.** *It's where creativity is born, where innovation thrives, and where new possibilities unfold. It's the space where you can reimagine yourself and your life without the constraints of past experiences, judgments, or limitations. And yes, it's also where the most profound lessons lie.*

*But how do you overcome the fear of the unknown? It starts with shifting your perspective. Instead of seeing uncertainty as a threat, start viewing it as an opportunity. Ask yourself:* **What would my life look like if I didn't fear the unknown?What could I create if I gave myself the freedom to explore without the weight of fear holding me back?**

*One powerful way to do this is by breaking the journey down into smaller, more manageable steps. The fear of the unknown often feels overwhelming because we see the whole journey as one giant leap into the abyss. But in reality, it's a series of small steps that lead to massive change.* **Each step you take diminishes the power of fear.** *The more you act, the more the unknown becomes known. It's the act of moving forward that transforms uncertainty into confidence.*

*Another important element in overcoming the fear of the unknown is building self-trust. The more you trust yourself to handle whatever comes your way, the less power fear has over you.* **Believe in your ability to adapt, to learn, and to grow.** *Trust that, no matter what happens, you will be okay. And when you trust yourself, the unknown loses its power to intimidate you. It becomes just another part of the adventure—an invitation to explore, to stretch, and to evolve.*

*The fear of the unknown will never fully disappear.* **It's part of the human experience.** *But the key is not to let it control you. Don't let it be the reason you* stay stuck. Don't let it be the excuse for not taking the leap. Instead, let it be the spark that ignites your courage and your drive to push beyond your limits. Let it remind you that the most incredible moments of your life are often waiting just outside your comfort zone.

The unknown is not something to fear. It's something to chase. Because within that unknown, you'll find **the person you are meant to become** and the life you are meant to live.

## 3. The Cost of Compliance

Living in constant pursuit of the expectations of others is a silent kind of surrender, a surrender that chips away at your soul little by little. It starts small—agreeing to things you don't really want to do, suppressing desires that don't align with what's expected of you, making compromises to please others. Over time, these small sacrifices begin to accumulate, forming a pattern that becomes harder and harder to break. Eventually, you realize you've lost more than just moments—you've lost parts of yourself.

The cost of compliance isn't always visible at first. It doesn't show up as an obvious sacrifice like financial loss or personal failure. Instead, it manifests as a slow, creeping emptiness, a sense of disconnection from who you really are. You might achieve everything *you thought you should—graduating with honors, landing the perfect job, building a successful career, maintaining healthy relationships—but when you look inside, there's a gnawing feeling that something is missing. You've played by the rules, followed the script, but you're left feeling unfulfilled, as if the life you've built isn't truly yours.*

*It's easy to convince yourself that the sacrifices are worth it—that you're doing what's necessary for success or happiness. But when you constantly bend yourself to fit into the mold others have set for you, you begin to lose your sense of purpose. **You end up living a life that was designed for someone else, not the one you truly desire.** You might find yourself working in a career you never truly wanted, staying in relationships that drain you, or following a path that others paved, not knowing how to create your own.*

*This process of compliance can be so gradual that it sneaks up on you. The first time you suppress a desire, you might feel a slight twinge of discomfort. The second time, it feels easier. By the time you've done it a hundred times, you no longer recognize the parts of you that have disappeared along the way. **You start to forget what you even wanted in the first place.** It's like trying to look at a picture through a foggy lens—while the outline of your life is still there, the details are blurred, and the color is lost.*

*The cost of compliance doesn't just affect your happiness—it also impacts your mental and emotional* *well-being. Constantly living according to someone else's expectations creates an internal conflict. **You're not being true to yourself**. This misalignment causes stress, anxiety, and burnout. The stress of pretending to be something you're not, the anxiety of not knowing if your choices are truly yours, and the burnout from giving more of yourself than you have to give can be overwhelming. And over time, this emotional exhaustion starts to take a toll on your physical health as well. **Your body starts to feel the weight of the compromises**. Fatigue, headaches, sleepless nights, and even chronic illnesses can manifest as the result of years spent disregarding your own needs and desires.*

*But the most damaging cost of compliance is the loss of your true self. You may begin to feel like a shell of the person you once were, disconnected from your passions, your dreams, and your purpose. You might look back on the years spent meeting the expectations of others and wonder where your individuality went. The person you see in the mirror doesn't reflect the vibrant, passionate soul you once were—it's someone who has been shaped by others, someone who has molded themselves to fit the roles they've been handed.*

*Here's the painful truth: **The price of compliance is your freedom**. Every time you say yes to someone else's desires and ignore your own, you hand over a piece of your autonomy. You give away your ability to choose for yourself, your ability to decide what matters most, and your ability to live authentically.*

*The more you comply with the expectations of others, the more you let go of your personal power. And in the end, this loss of freedom leads to a life that feels like it's on autopilot—a life that moves forward without your full presence, without your full engagement.*

*But here's the good news: it doesn't have to stay this way.* **Breaking free from the chains of compliance is possible.** *It begins with awareness—the realization that you have been living according to someone else's script, and that this script doesn't define who you are or who you want to become. Once you recognize this, you can begin to make different choices. The first step is to ask yourself:* **What do I really want? What makes me feel alive? What does my heart truly desire?** *It's time to start listening to your inner voice, the one that has been drowned out by the noise of others' expectations.*

*As you begin to tune into your own desires, you might feel resistance. It's natural to fear disappointing others or stepping away from familiar patterns. But* **the truth is, you can't make everyone happy.** *Not everyone will understand or support your decision to live authentically, but that's okay. The people who truly care for you will respect your journey toward self-discovery, even if it means you no longer fit into the role they once imagined for you.* **Living for yourself, not for others, is the key to reclaiming your freedom and your happiness.**

*The cost of compliance is high, but so is the cost of never living the life you were meant to live. The choice is yours. Will you continue to live for others, or will you finally choose to live for yourself?*

## 4. Breaking Free

*Breaking free from the weight of others' expectations is one of the most liberating—and difficult—things you can do for yourself. It's not just about saying no to the things that drain you or letting go of relationships that no longer serve you. It's about taking back control over your life and stepping into your own power. It's about choosing authenticity, even when it's easier to follow the crowd. Breaking free is an act of radical self-love, and it's the first step toward creating a life that truly reflects who you are.*

*To break free from the chains of compliance, you need to start with awareness.* **You must first recognize the forces that have shaped you**—*the societal norms, family expectations, the well-meaning advice of others, and even the subtle pressures that influence your choices. These external forces have been guiding your decisions for far too long, but now, it's time to ask yourself:* **What do I truly want? What do I believe in? What makes me feel alive?**

*The journey to freedom begins with self-awareness. It's about getting in touch with your inner desires, your values, and your passions.* **You can't break free** *from something if you don't know what it is you're trying to break free to. You need to get clear on what your authentic life looks like, not the one that was designed by others.*

*Start by tuning out the noise of external influences. Take time to reflect on your life, without the weight of others' opinions. **Ask yourself: If no one expected anything from me, what would I do? What would I change about my life if I could start fresh?** It's vital to give yourself permission to dream, even if those dreams don't fit neatly into the box society has drawn for you.*

*Once you have clarity, the next step is to challenge the limiting beliefs that have kept you bound. These beliefs are often so ingrained in our thinking that we don't even realize they are there. **You may believe that you're not good enough to pursue your dreams, or that you need to conform to be accepted.** These beliefs hold you back, keeping you stuck in patterns that no longer serve you.*

*To break free, you need to consciously confront these limiting beliefs and replace them with empowering truths. **You are worthy of pursuing your dreams, regardless of whether others understand or approve. You don't need anyone's permission to live authentically.** It's your life, and you are the only one who gets to define it. Challenge the narratives that say you can't do something because of where you come from, what others expect, or what you think is* *possible.*

*Breaking free also requires you to learn how to disappoint others. This may be one of the hardest parts of the process. The people around you—family, friends, colleagues—may have their own expectations of what you should do, how you should behave, and who you should become. But here's the reality:* **Not everyone will understand your need for independence, and that's okay.** *The people who truly care about you will respect your decision to live authentically, even if it means you no longer fit into the role they once imagined for you. You are not here to fulfill the expectations of others; you are here to fulfill your own potential.*

*Learning to disappoint others isn't about being selfish or unkind—it's about prioritizing your own well-being and happiness.* **If you're constantly worried about disappointing people, you'll never be able to live your truth.** *It's a hard truth to accept, but it's necessary for growth. The more you honor your own desires and needs, the less you will feel the weight of others' expectations. And over time, you will become more comfortable with making choices that align with your heart, even if they don't always make everyone else happy.*

*Another critical aspect of breaking free is setting boundaries. Boundaries are not just about saying no to others—they are about saying yes to yourself.* **They are the lines you draw to protect your energy, your**

**time, and your emotional well-being.** *Without boundaries, it's easy to fall into the trap of saying yes to everything, of constantly giving to others without leaving anything for yourself. But when you learn to set boundaries, you take back control of your life. You give yourself permission to prioritize your own needs and dreams.*

*Setting boundaries can be uncomfortable at first. People may resist, and you may fear their judgment. But remember:* **You have the right to protect your peace and to create a life that is meaningful to you.** *Setting boundaries doesn't mean you are being harsh or uncaring—it means you are protecting your ability to show up as the best version of yourself.*

*Breaking free also means taking action. Freedom doesn't come from just thinking about change—it comes from* **deciding to make a move, however small, in the direction of your dreams.** *It means taking that first step, even when the path ahead seems unclear. It's easy to feel overwhelmed by the enormity of the change you want to make, but don't let that stop you. The key to breaking free is consistency—making small, deliberate steps toward your authentic life, every single day. Over time, these small steps add up to monumental change.*

*Finally, breaking free requires patience. It's a process, not a one-time event. There will be setbacks, there will be moments when you doubt yourself, and there will be times when you feel the pressure of society's expectations bearing down on you. But in those moments, remember this:* **You are worth the effort it takes to break free.** *Your dreams, your happiness, and your peace of mind are worth fighting for.*

*Breaking free isn't easy, but it is the most rewarding thing you can do for yourself. It's a choice to live for yourself, to create the life you want, not the life others expect. It's a choice to live authentically and unapologetically. And when you make that choice, you will find that the world opens up to you in ways you never imagined.*

## 5. Moving Forward

*Walking away from what no longer serves you is just the first step. It's a powerful, liberating decision, but the real transformation happens when you start moving forward. Moving forward isn't just about leaving something behind; it's about* **creating space for something new,** *something better. It's about rediscovering who you are and what you truly want in life. It's about embracing the unknown, letting go of the past, and stepping boldly into the future with a renewed sense of purpose.*

*Once you've let go of what was holding you back,* **the next phase of your journey is about rebuilding your life in a way that feels aligned with your authentic self.** *It's not just about filling the void left by what you've left behind, but about creating a life that is* *richer, fuller, and more meaningful.*

*One of the most important aspects of moving forward is **rediscovering yourself**. When you let go of old expectations, societal pressures, and relationships that no longer serve you, you create space to reconnect with your true self. For many people, this can feel like a process of reawakening. **You might feel like you've lost touch with who you are, especially after years of living according to someone else's script.** Moving forward requires you to take the time to reflect on your values, your passions, and what truly brings you joy.*

***Take a step back and ask yourself: What makes me feel alive? What activities or moments have sparked joy in my life?** Reconnect with those things. Whether it's a creative hobby you've abandoned, a passion you've ignored, or a goal you've pushed aside, now is the time to pursue what speaks to your soul. **No matter how small or insignificant these things may seem, they are a part of you**—and they hold the key to your fulfillment. Rediscovering what excites you allows you to start moving forward with a sense of purpose and clarity.*

*As you move forward, **it's important to set new boundaries.** The boundaries you set in the past were likely designed to protect you from people or situations that no longer felt right. But now, as you create a new chapter in your life, your boundaries should evolve with you. **Boundaries are not just about protecting yourself—they are about*** *protecting the life you are building. They are the limits you set to preserve your energy, time, and emotional well-being.*

*Start by identifying what you want to say "yes" to moving forward. What kind of people, experiences, and opportunities do you want to invite into your life? And just as importantly, **decide what you are willing to say "no" to**. Saying no is not about rejecting others; it's about choosing yourself. It's about making decisions that honor your well-being, goals, and vision for the future.*

***The next step is to cultivate self-compassion**. It's easy to get caught up in the rush of moving forward, to feel like you need to have everything figured out immediately. But remember, **healing takes time**, and so does rebuilding. Moving forward is not a linear path—it's a journey, and sometimes that journey includes setbacks, self-doubt, and moments of vulnerability. And that's okay. What matters is that you keep going, even on the days when it feels tough.*

*You may face moments of loneliness as you move forward, and that's normal. Letting go of relationships or environments that no longer serve you can create a sense of emptiness. But instead of seeing this as a negative, **view it as an opportunity to reconnect with yourself**. Use this time to nurture your own growth, to explore your inner world, and to develop a deeper understanding of who you are. **When you learn to be comfortable in your own company,*** *you unlock the potential to build stronger, healthier relationships in the future.*

*Another critical aspect of moving forward is **embracing change.** Change can be uncomfortable, especially if you've spent a long time in a place that no longer aligns with your true self. But change is necessary for growth. **To move forward, you need to let go of the past and embrace the uncertainty of the future.** Trust that as you step into the unknown, the universe will align the right opportunities and people to support you along the way. **Change is not something to fear—it's something to welcome.***

*As you move forward, **set new goals** that align with your authentic self. Think beyond what you were told you should want and focus on what truly lights you up. Whether it's pursuing a new career, starting a new creative project, traveling, or building new relationships, moving forward gives you the freedom to set goals that are meaningful to you. **Your dreams are yours to create, and now that you've made space for them, it's time to actively pursue them.***

***Stay open to new experiences***. *Moving forward isn't just about focusing on the destination—it's about embracing the journey. The more open you are to the unknown, the more opportunities will come your way. Whether it's meeting new people, learning new skills, or stepping out of your comfort zone, each new experience will shape you into the person you are meant to become.*

*Finally,* **trust yourself.** *After all the work it takes to let go, rebuild, and redefine your life, the most important thing is to trust your intuition. Your instincts are your guiding compass.* **You don't need to have all the answers right now.** *Trust that as you continue to move forward, you will be guided in the right direction. You've already proven that you are strong enough to walk away from what no longer serves you, and now you need to trust that the path you are forging is the one meant for you.*

*Moving forward is the culmination of all the hard work you've put in to reclaim your power. It's about trusting that by choosing yourself and creating a life that is true to who you are, you are not just surviving—you are thriving.* **And with every step you take toward your true self, you create a life that is rich, fulfilling, and deeply yours.**

*As you step forward, leaving behind what no longer serves you, remember that* **the journey is far from over.** *The road ahead may be uncharted, and at times, it may feel like the weight of the world is on your* *shoulders. But with every step you take, you move closer to your true self. And while the road may seem long,* **it's important to remember that your dreams are not bound by time or circumstance.**

**"A man's dream is his own, and no one can take that from him." — Blackbeard**

*Your dreams are not just a destination—they are an endless horizon, a continual evolution of who you are and who you are becoming.* **There is no final end to your dreams, only the next chapter, the next goal, the next step forward.** *Your dream is a living thing, it grows with you, shifts with you, and will continue to push you to new heights, even when you think you've reached your peak.*

**"People's dreams have no end." — Blackbeard**

*This is the truth about dreams—they are endless.* **No matter where you are in life, no matter what you've achieved or where you've been, your dreams will always have room to grow, to expand, and to evolve.** *Dreams are not bound by time or circumstance; they are a part of your soul, always pushing you toward your next horizon.*

*Every challenge, every moment of doubt, every setback is part of your dream's expansion.* **Your dreams are not limited—they are infinite, as long as you are** *willing* **to keep going, to keep evolving, to keep believing.** *So don't ever stop dreaming. Keep pushing forward, keep evolving, and trust that every step, no matter how small, brings you closer to a version of yourself you've yet to meet.*

*Remember,* **the only thing that can truly stop you from achieving your dreams is yourself.** *Keep walking, keep dreaming, and know that the journey is endless. The world is yours to shape, and your dreams will carry you forward, always.*

*Your dream is more than just a fleeting thought. It's a calling. A whisper in your soul that asks you to take action. It's not a path that's always easy, but it's the path that will bring you the most fulfillment.* **Don't let fear, doubt, or the expectations of others hold you back.** *Follow your dream with everything you have, and you'll find that the universe will conspire to help you along the way.*

*The only question left is:* **Are you ready to take that first step?**

*"Dreams are the whispers of the soul, and as long as you listen, they will guide you toward a future that has no end."*

## CHAPTER TWELVE

# THE BEAUTY OF IMPERFECTION

## 1. The Pressure of Perfection

*From the moment we take our first breath, we are bombarded with the unspoken pressures of perfection. Whether we realize it or not, the world around us begins to shape our perception of what success, happiness, and worth should look like. We grow up with messages about what we should wear, how we should act, what career we should pursue, and even who we should love. These ideas, expectations, and standards form an invisible script that we are expected to follow.*

*In school, we are told to get good grades, excel in extracurriculars, and ultimately get into the best universities. In our families, we might feel the pressure to make our parents proud, to achieve milestones they deem important, and to live up to their ideals. Society, through its obsession with perfect appearances and flawless lives, whispers that we should always be better, smarter, richer, and more successful. But who decided these standards? Who wrote the rulebook we're expected to follow?*

*Think about it for a second—how many times have you found yourself striving for something that wasn't necessarily something you wanted, but something you were told you needed? A career path that didn't excite you, a certain look that wasn't authentic, or relationships that weren't fulfilling—yet you pushed through because you believed this was what was expected of you.*

*The truth is, we have all been conditioned to chase perfection. And in doing so, we begin to internalize these outside expectations, believing that our worth is tied to our ability to meet them. We become so focused on attaining an idealized version of success that we forget what it feels like to simply be. We forget to check in with ourselves and ask: "Is this really what I want, or is it what the world says I should want?"*

*You've likely experienced the pressure of perfection at some point in your life. Maybe it was the pressure to get straight A's in school or to be the perfect friend, the perfect partner, or the perfect employee. And while striving for excellence can be motivating and healthy in moderation, perfectionism breeds anxiety, stress, and feelings of inadequacy. You might have pushed yourself to the limit, trying to meet everyone's expectations, only to find yourself exhausted, burned out, or unsatisfied.*

*It's easy to get trapped in the idea that the only way to be valued is through perfection. But what if perfection is a lie? What if it's a mask that prevents us from showing the world our true, imperfect selves?*

*You've probably seen those curated images on social media—flawless people, perfect lives, and picture-perfect moments. You might have felt like you had to keep up with that standard, that somehow, your imperfections weren't enough. You might have compared your reality to someone else's highlight reel and felt like you were falling short. But here's the reality: those pictures, those moments—they are carefully crafted, staged, and often far removed from the truth. Behind every "perfect" image is a person, just like you, with their own struggles, imperfections, and dreams.*

*So, why do we continue to chase this unattainable ideal? Why do we pressure ourselves to measure up to something that doesn't truly exist?*

*The answer lies in a deep-seated fear—the fear of not being enough. We fear that if we don't meet the standards set by others, we'll be judged, rejected, or overlooked. But what if I told you that the very thing we fear is also the thing that holds us back from our true potential?*

*The pressure of perfection is a lie. It's a heavy weight that weighs us down, preventing us from embracing who we really are. It keeps us trapped in a cycle of self-criticism, doubt, and endless striving. But what if we decided to let go of that pressure? What if we allowed ourselves to breathe, to make mistakes, and to embrace imperfection?*

*The moment you begin to question the narrative of perfection and start living authentically, you take your first step toward freedom. Let go of the need to be flawless. It's okay to be messy, to make mistakes, and to not have it all figured out. In fact, it's in these moments of imperfection where you will find your true power—your authenticity.*

**To the reader who feels the weight of perfection on their shoulders: You are not alone.**

*You don't have to be perfect. You don't have to conform to anyone's idea of success. Your worth isn't determined by how well you perform or how perfectly you live your life. Your value comes from within, from who you are at your core, imperfections and all. When you stop chasing perfection, you give yourself the gift of peace and acceptance. And in that peace, you can finally breathe freely, knowing that you are enough, just as you are.*

## 2. The Silent Pressure

*Expectations are not always loud. Sometimes, the pressure is silent—an unspoken weight that rests heavily on our shoulders without us even realizing it. It's in the subtle glances, the gentle nudges, and the societal whispers that tell us how we should live, what we should believe, and who we should become. These pressures often creep into our lives without warning, shaping the way we think, act, and interact with the world.*

*It starts innocently enough—comments from well-meaning family members or friends. "Why don't you settle down yet?" "When are you going to get that promotion?" "You're really good at that; you should pursue it more seriously." At first, these comments may seem harmless, but over time, they add up, creating a growing list of expectations that don't necessarily align with our true desires. We start to internalize the belief that we should meet others' standards, that their ideas of success are the only valid ones.*

*But what happens when the world around us tells us who we should be, and we listen? What happens when we start to measure our worth against these silent pressures, without even fully understanding where they come from?*

*The silent pressure doesn't always appear in the form of direct commands. Often, it's the societal norms that dictate what success looks like—the invisible timeline of life that tells us when to get married, when to buy a house, when to have kids, or when we should be at the peak of our career. We watch those around us, and we think that we should be at the same stage. We get caught in the comparison trap, believing that we need to follow the same path.*

*The quiet, unspoken expectations can come from social media too. With the rise of curated feeds and polished portrayals of lives, we often feel like we need to keep up. We see the perfectly filtered lives of others, and we begin to question if we are enough, if we're doing enough, or if we're "behind" in life. Everyone else seems to have it all together—why can't we?*

*The worst part about this silent pressure is that it's often self-inflicted. We begin to set these standards for ourselves based on what others are doing, not based on what we genuinely want. We feel like we must meet these invisible deadlines or face judgment, even if the timelines and milestones don't align with our unique journey.*

*Have you ever stopped and thought about the weight of these silent pressures? Have you ever realized how much of what you're striving for is based on what others expect from you, rather than what you truly want for yourself?*

*It's easy to get lost in this cycle, thinking that you're simply living up to expectations. But deep down, many of us feel a lingering sense of dissatisfaction. The reason? You're not living for yourself; you're living for others' approval. When you do this, you begin to lose sight of who you are, what you truly want, and where you are headed in life. The pressure builds, and before you know it, you're overwhelmed, burnt out, and disconnected from your true self.*

*Think about the times you've felt unfulfilled or exhausted. Was it because you weren't achieving enough? Or was it because you were chasing someone else's idea of success? It's important to reflect on this, because the more you live under the silent pressure of meeting others' expectations, the further you drift from your authentic self.*

*Here's the hard truth: **The silent pressure will never stop.** It will always be there in some form, waiting for you to meet someone else's standards. But it's up to you to decide if you're going to continue to live under that pressure or if you're going to break free.*

*It takes courage to listen to your own voice and tune out the noise. It takes strength to walk away from the pressures that don't serve you and to live a life based on your own values and desires, not the ones others have set for you. You don't owe anyone a version of your life that doesn't align with who you truly are.*

*Remember, it's okay to disappoint others. It's okay if people don't understand your choices. They are not living your life, you are. And if you choose to prioritize your own happiness and fulfillment, you are doing the most courageous thing you can do for yourself.*

*To truly step into your power, you must begin by acknowledging these silent pressures and taking control of your narrative. Stop comparing yourself to others and start comparing yourself to who you were yesterday. Your journey is uniquely yours, and it's time to stop living for anyone else's approval.*

***You are not here to meet the expectations of others.*** *You are here to create your own path, to live authentically, and to follow your own dreams, regardless of the silent pressure society places on you. Let go of the weight of others' opinions and start living a life that is true to you.*

## 3. The Cost of Compliance

*We've all been there—making decisions that aren't truly ours, conforming to expectations that don't align with our authentic selves. At first, it seems harmless enough. "This is just what I have to do," you might think. "Everyone else is doing it, so why shouldn't I?" But over time, the cost of compliance adds up, and it comes at a price higher than we realize. The toll it takes on our mental, emotional, and physical well-being is often overlooked, and the consequences can be deeply damaging.*

*At its core, living up to someone else's expectations means sacrificing pieces of yourself in order to fit into a mold that wasn't designed for you. Every time you silence your own desires, you lose a bit of who you are. Every time you push aside your passion or your authentic truth to meet the demands of others, you trade your inner peace for temporary approval.*

*The worst part is that the cost doesn't always show up immediately. In the beginning, you might feel like you're succeeding. You get the promotion, you meet the milestones, and you check all the boxes. But slowly, imperceptibly, you begin to feel something is missing. You might feel like you've accomplished everything you were told to do—graduate, land a job, settle down—but somehow, you're still empty inside.*

*That emptiness? It's the cost of living someone else's life.*

*We live in a world that is obsessed with outward success—titles, awards, the size of your paycheck, how many followers you have. These external markers are often used to measure worth, but they fail to account for the most important aspect of our existence: our internal well-being. When you measure your value based solely on what society tells you is important, you disconnect from what truly matters to you.*

*The more you comply with external expectations, the further you drift from your true desires and the things that make you feel alive. You start living for the approval of others, whether it's your parents, your boss, or your peers. But approval is fleeting—it doesn't sustain you the way self-acceptance and inner fulfillment do.*

*You may find yourself trapped in a cycle where you work harder to please others, but the harder you work, the more exhausted and drained you feel. You keep achieving, but you're running on empty. The toll on your mental health is immense, and before you know it, you're not just physically drained—you're emotionally and spiritually depleted.*

***Think about the times you've felt burnt out, stressed, or overwhelmed.*** *Were you running after someone else's dream for your life? Were you trying to meet a standard that wasn't even yours to begin with? The more you comply with external demands, the more you suppress your own needs, desires, and dreams. This creates a deep sense of* *dissatisfaction—a nagging feeling that something is off, even if you don't quite know what it is.*

*What's even more dangerous is that the longer you stay on this path, the harder it becomes to break free. You begin to lose touch with your own voice, your own desires, and your own truth. Over time, you start to question whether you even know what you really want anymore.*

*But there's a critical point you can reach—a point where you realize that the cost is too high. You can no longer afford to keep ignoring your own needs. You can no longer sacrifice your happiness, your passion, and your authenticity just to meet someone else's expectations.*

***It's important to recognize that you have a choice.*** *You don't have to keep sacrificing yourself for the sake of others' approval. Yes, it's scary. Yes, it may feel uncomfortable at first. But the moment you begin to honor your true desires, you will start to feel a shift inside you. You'll feel lighter, freer, and more aligned with who you really are.*

*What happens when you stop living for others' approval?* ***You start living for yourself.*** *You start making decisions based on what brings you joy, what excites you, and what aligns with your purpose. You begin to honor your own needs, and in doing so, you unlock a level of peace and fulfillment that's* impossible to achieve when you're chasing someone else's dream.

It's not just about letting go of the expectations of others—it's about reclaiming your life. It's about making room for what truly matters to you, regardless of how others may react. Yes, people will be disappointed. Yes, some will judge. But in the end, **the only opinion that truly matters is yours.**

So, the next time you find yourself wondering why you're feeling drained, unfulfilled, or disconnected, take a step back and ask yourself: **Whose life am I living?**

And if it's not your own, **it's time to make a change.** You deserve a life that reflects your true desires, your true passions, and your true self. Let go of the expectations, and begin living on your own terms.

The cost of compliance is steep, but the price of reclaiming your life? **It's worth everything.**

### 4. Breaking Free

Breaking free from the chains of expectations is one of the most powerful acts of self-liberation you can undertake. It's not just about walking away from a job, a relationship, or a lifestyle that no longer serves *you—it's about breaking free from the mental, emotional, and societal constraints that have been placed upon you. It's about reconnecting with who you truly are and what you truly desire, without the weight of everyone else's judgments and expectations.*

*But breaking free is never easy.* **It requires courage.** *Courage to confront the reality that not everyone will understand your choices. Courage to disappoint people, knowing that it's not about them—it's about you. Courage to face the discomfort of doing something different, even when you don't know what the future holds.*

*Many of us have been conditioned to believe that breaking free is selfish or irresponsible. We've been taught that we must always put others' needs before our own, that we should always conform, and that the path to success is paved with sacrifices—sacrifices of our time, our happiness, and even our integrity. But* **the truth is that you cannot live a fulfilled life by constantly sacrificing your own well-being for others' comfort.**

*Breaking free starts with a shift in perspective.* **It's about seeing your needs as just as valid and important as anyone else's.** *You deserve to live a life that resonates with your core values, not one dictated by societal standards. The first step is to identify the areas where you are holding yourself back.*

*Are you staying in a job that drains you because it's what others expect? Are you in a relationship that no longer aligns with who you are because you're afraid of letting someone down? Are you living your life according to an outdated script that's no longer true for you?*

*The moment you start questioning those areas is the moment you begin to break free. It's about looking at the things in your life and saying, "Does this truly align with who I am? Does this support my happiness and growth?" If the answer is no, it's time to let go.*

***It's okay to outgrow things.*** *It's okay to let go of relationships, careers, or environments that no longer align with your evolving self. And just because something has been a part of your life for a long time doesn't mean it's meant to stay forever. People change. Priorities shift. Life moves forward. You are allowed to change along with it.*

*But breaking free doesn't mean quitting everything or running away from challenges.* ***It means making a conscious choice to move toward what truly supports you.*** *It means stepping away from the things that drain you and stepping toward the things that replenish you. It means learning to set boundaries, even when others resist them. It means giving yourself permission to say no—to say no to situations that rob you of your peace, your energy, and your joy.*

*When you begin to break free, you'll notice a shift in your energy. You'll feel lighter, more aligned, and more connected to your true self. You'll begin to make decisions that honor your desires, your values, and your purpose. And although the journey may feel uncertain and uncomfortable at first, the discomfort is only temporary.* **It's the discomfort of growth—of shedding old layers that no longer serve you and stepping into a new, more authentic version of yourself.**

*At first, it may seem like everything is falling apart. Relationships might become strained. People might question your decisions. But remember this:* **letting go of what doesn't serve you is the first step to creating space for what does.** *And when you let go of the things that are holding you back, you open yourself up to new opportunities, experiences, and people who are in alignment with your true self.*

*Breaking free also means letting go of* **guilt.** *Too many people hold themselves back because they feel guilty for taking care of themselves or for choosing their own path.* **But guilt is a tool that keeps you stuck.** *It's a mechanism used by society, by other people, and sometimes even by your own inner critic, to keep you compliant and small. When you break free, you have to release that guilt and remind yourself that* **you are not responsible for anyone else's happiness but your own.**

*In fact, by staying in situations that no longer serve you just to keep others comfortable, you're actually doing a disservice to both yourself and them. The people who truly care about you want you to live a life that makes you happy and fulfilled—not a life that meets their expectations at the cost of your own well-being.*

*Breaking free isn't an event—it's a process.* **It's a series of small, deliberate choices to prioritize your own growth and happiness over external validation.** *It's about taking the leap, even when you're unsure of where you'll land. It's about having the courage to trust that once you let go of the things that no longer serve you, the universe will fill the void with something better.*

**And it's okay to take that first step, no matter how small.** *Even if you're not sure what the next chapter looks like, taking one step toward breaking free is already progress. That's where true freedom begins—the moment you choose yourself over the expectations of others.*

*So, take a moment and ask yourself:* **What do I need to break free from?**

*Is it an outdated belief? A toxic relationship? A job that drains your soul? Whatever it is, give yourself permission to release it. It's your birthright to live a life that reflects who you truly are, not who others want you to be.*

*And when you do break free, don't look back with regret. Look forward with excitement, because **the life you've been waiting for is waiting for you, too.***

## 5. Living on Your Own Terms

*Living on your own terms is the ultimate form of personal freedom. It's not just about making decisions that reflect your values, it's about owning your choices, embracing your individuality, and learning how to say no to the things that don't serve you. When you live on your own terms, you take control of your life, your actions, and your future.*

*But what does it mean to truly live on your own terms? It's about breaking free from the prison of other people's expectations and stepping into a life that reflects your deepest desires and passions. It's about learning how to honor your needs without feeling guilty or apologetic. It's about living authentically, even when it's uncomfortable or unpopular.*

*Living on your own terms isn't about being rebellious for the sake of rebellion. **It's about alignment.** It's about aligning your daily actions with the person you want to be and the life you want to live. It's about making decisions that come from within, not from the outside world. It's about choosing what brings* *you peace, joy, and fulfillment, even if those choices challenge the status quo.*

*When you begin to live on your own terms, you start to notice something powerful—it feels like breathing fresh air after being suffocated. The weight of societal pressure begins to lift, and you begin to feel lighter, more confident, and more connected to your authentic self. You realize that you don't need anyone's permission to live your life the way you want to.*

*The first step toward living on your own terms is* **clarity.** *You have to get clear on what you want. So many people are caught in a cycle of pleasing others, that they forget to ask themselves, What do I truly want for my life? And it's okay if the answer isn't immediately clear—this is a process. You might need time to reflect, to experiment, to fail, and to grow.*

*Ask yourself:*

- *What makes me come alive?*

- *What do I value most in life?*

- *What goals do I have that are purely mine, not influenced by anyone else?*

•

*What would I do if I knew there were no limits?*

*Getting clear on your desires and values is essential because, once you know what truly matters to you, the path to living on your own terms becomes much more straightforward. You'll be able to say no to the things that don't align with your truth, and yes to the things that will nourish your soul.*

*One of the most important aspects of living on your own terms is learning to **set boundaries.** Boundaries are an essential tool for protecting your peace and ensuring that you don't lose yourself in the expectations and demands of others. Setting boundaries is not about being rigid or unkind—it's about protecting your energy and maintaining your sense of self.*

***Boundaries aren't walls.** They're more like fences, marking the line between you and others. They help you define where you end and where others begin. When you set clear boundaries, you let people know what you will and won't tolerate, what is acceptable and what isn't.*

*But setting boundaries can be uncomfortable at first. You may feel guilty, especially if you're used to pleasing others. But remember, **you can't pour from an empty cup.** If you constantly give and give without* *replenishing yourself, you will eventually burn out. Setting boundaries allows you to conserve your energy and focus on the things that matter most to you.*

*Another crucial element of living on your own terms is* **embracing imperfection.** *When you stop trying to be perfect, you open yourself up to a world of possibility. Perfectionism is a form of self-sabotage—it keeps you stuck in fear and prevents you from taking risks. It keeps you from stepping into the arena of life and pursuing your dreams. But perfection is a myth.*

*Living on your own terms means allowing yourself to make mistakes, to learn from them, and to grow. It means embracing the messy, imperfect parts of life and accepting that you will never have everything figured out. And that's okay.* **Progress is better than perfection.**

*When you stop holding yourself to impossible standards, you free yourself to try new things, explore different paths, and make choices that are aligned with who you truly are. The beauty of living on your own terms is that* **you get to create your own rules.** *You get to define success on your own terms, without comparing yourself to anyone else.*

*Living authentically doesn't always mean easy decisions or smooth paths. In fact, it can often mean making choices that are difficult, unconventional, or unpopular. But the reward is a life that feels true to you—a life where you are proud of the person you are becoming, not because of external validation, but because you've stayed true to yourself.*

***Living on your own terms is a journey, not a destination.*** *It's a daily practice of choosing yourself, of saying no to things that no longer serve you, and of saying yes to the things that set your soul on fire. And, when you begin to live authentically, you will begin to attract people and opportunities that resonate with your truth.*

*No one else gets to write your story. You are the author, and every decision you make is a new chapter.* ***Live in a way that makes you proud of the life you're creating.***

*It's time to stop living for others and start living for yourself.* ***Live the life that sets you free.***

*Living on your own terms isn't just a choice; it's a declaration. It's a decision to honor yourself in a world that constantly tries to tell you who to be. It's about finding the courage to step into your own power, to follow your heart, and to trust that the path you choose is the right one—for you.*

*As you step forward, don't be afraid to make mistakes. The beauty of living authentically is that you get to redefine success on your own terms. With every step, you move closer to becoming the person you were always meant to be.*

*Remember, **true freedom comes when you stop seeking permission to be yourself.** When you let go of other people's expectations and embrace your own truth, you open up a world of endless possibilities. It's not about the destination; it's about the journey of self-discovery, growth, and living a life that feels aligned with your soul.*

*And as you navigate the twists and turns of life, remember this:*

**"The most beautiful life is one where you're free to be exactly who you are, with no apologies and no regrets."**

## CHAPTER THIRTEEN

# THE FEAR OF MISSING OUT (FOMO) AND THE POWER OF PRESENCE

**What is FOMO?**

**The Rise of FOMO: A Modern Epidemic**

*Have you ever found yourself scrolling through social media, mindlessly checking the latest posts, and suddenly felt a sinking sensation in your stomach? A feeling that others are out there living their best lives, experiencing things you wish you were a part of? That's FOMO—The Fear of Missing Out.*

*FOMO is a psychological phenomenon that's become almost synonymous with our modern, connected world. In an age where we can see everyone else's curated highlight reel in real-time, it's easy to start feeling like you're being left behind. You begin to compare yourself to others—people who seem to have it all together, with perfect vacations, relationships, or careers. And in that comparison, you might start questioning your own life. "Why am I not doing that?" or "Am I missing out on something?" These questions can take root, and suddenly, it feels like you're not measuring up.*

**But here's the truth: FOMO isn't just about what's happening around you. It's about how you perceive the world.** *It's about looking at someone else's success or fun, and thinking that your own life doesn't measure up. The irony? That same sense of "missing out" can distract us from fully appreciating what we do have in the present moment.*

**The Psychological Toll of FOMO**

*FOMO is not just a fleeting feeling—it's an emotional and mental battle. It's a constant undercurrent of anxiety, driving you to stay connected, to keep up with every trend, every event, every conversation. With the rise of social media, FOMO has become a pervasive force in our daily lives. Platforms like Instagram, Twitter, and Facebook offer instant access to everyone's best moments, making it hard not to feel like you're missing something important.*

*The psychological toll of FOMO is real. Studies have shown that constantly being exposed to the "best" moments of others can cause feelings of inadequacy and even depression. The human brain isn't designed to process the sheer volume of information we're fed through social media, and the constant comparison doesn't help. It leads to anxiety, and a cycle of wanting more, feeling less, and never truly being content with where you are.*

*But it's important to remember: FOMO isn't necessarily about what you're lacking. It's about the disconnect between what you think you should have and what's actually happening in your life. And when we start chasing that "perfect life" we see online, we can easily lose sight of the beauty and depth of our own lives.*

**The Real FOMO: Fear of Missing Yourself**

*FOMO doesn't always come from external influences—it can also stem from our internal desires and fears. Sometimes, we fear missing out on the person we could be, the experiences we could have, or the relationships we could form. The question becomes: Are you trying to live a life for others, or are you trying to build a life that resonates with you?*

*Here's where we get to the heart of the issue. FOMO isn't just about what you're not doing—it's about the life you're not living because you're so busy looking at everyone else's. The power of this chapter isn't in explaining what's wrong with FOMO. It's in realizing that we have the ability to stop chasing a life that isn't ours.* **We can choose presence over comparison.**

*The key to overcoming FOMO lies in the simple truth that you are enough, right where you are. It's about focusing on your own path and recognizing that your journey doesn't have to look like anyone else's. You're not falling behind. You're not missing out. You're simply living your own story—an important, unique one that doesn't need to be measured against anyone else's.*

### *Social Media's Role in FOMO*

*In today's world, social media plays a massive role in fueling FOMO. Instagram photos of exotic vacations, Facebook updates about life-changing events, and Twitter posts about exciting new opportunities create a narrative that everyone is out there doing amazing things. But behind the screens, there's a story we don't always see: the anxiety, the planning, the filters, and even the lonely moments that don't make it into those perfectly framed pictures. What you're seeing isn't the whole truth.*

*We're fed a version of reality that's been carefully curated, edited, and sometimes completely fabricated. This highlights the illusion of perfection and causes us to believe that everyone else is living their dream life while we're stuck in a routine. But here's the reality check—no one has it all together all the time. And social media, while connecting us, often distances us from the truth of our own lives.*

**Ask yourself: What would happen if you stepped away from the noise? What if you could find peace in your own life, free from the pressure of constant comparison?**

**A Call to Reflect: What's Truly Missing?**

*To move beyond FOMO, it's important to ask yourself, "What am I truly missing?" Is it the excitement, the adventure, or the validation? Or is it something deeper—the connection to your true self, the grounding in your own desires and values?*

*Instead of chasing others' experiences, ask yourself: What would bring true fulfillment to my life? What would make me feel truly alive and connected to the present moment?*

*Living for yourself, rather than constantly reacting to the outside world, is how we begin to reclaim our lives from FOMO. It's about becoming aware of the narratives you've been sold about what's "missing" and questioning whether those are truly the things that matter to you.*

## A Final Thought on FOMO

*You'll always see someone else doing something exciting, traveling somewhere new, or achieving something remarkable. But that doesn't mean you're falling behind. It simply means that their path is different from yours, and that's okay. You don't have to run at the same pace as everyone else.*

*Instead, learn to appreciate your own journey and recognize the unique opportunities you have in the present. Choose to live in your own moment—fully, deeply, and without the pull of comparison.*

*And remember:* **True fulfillment doesn't come from what we're missing—it comes from embracing what we have right now.**

## 2. The Illusion of Missing Out

### Chasing Perfection: The FOMO Mirage

*We've all been there. You scroll through your phone, and suddenly, the images and updates that pop up feel like a never-ending parade of "better" lives—vacations, weddings, career achievements, and social gatherings that seem more exciting than your current reality. You start to feel like you're missing something—like you're being left out of a perfect, ideal version of life that everyone else is living.*

*This is the illusion of missing out.*

*What you're really feeling isn't FOMO; it's a trick of the mind. The human brain has a tendency to overvalue what's in front of us, and in the case of social media, it often overvalues the lives of others. We start to believe that what we see online is the full, unfiltered truth. However, what we're really seeing is a snapshot of someone's curated life—a highlight reel, not the behind-the-scenes reality.*

***Here's the thing:*** *You don't know what's going on behind those perfectly framed photos. You don't know the challenges, struggles, or disappointments that come with those seemingly perfect moments. The "fun" vacation might have been filled with stress. The* *happy relationship might be hiding the complexities that come with it. And that "perfect" job may involve burnout or sacrifice that isn't showcased on Instagram. The illusion of missing out blinds you to the reality that everyone has their ups and downs, their highs and lows.*

## The Dangers of Comparison: The Thief of Joy

*When we compare ourselves to others, we're not comparing real lives; we're comparing idealized versions of those lives. It's easy to fall into the trap of thinking that everyone else is living a life of constant excitement and happiness, while we're stuck in a cycle of ordinary routines and struggles. This sense of being "left behind" is what fuels FOMO, but it's built on an unstable foundation of comparison.*

*Comparison is dangerous—it's the thief of joy. When you compare your "behind-the-scenes" to someone else's "highlight reel," you're setting yourself up for disappointment. Everyone has their own story, their own timeline, and their own challenges. No one's life is as perfect as it may seem on the outside. What you see in someone else's feed may not even be an accurate reflection of their reality.*

*In truth, comparison not only makes you feel inadequate but also leads to dissatisfaction and self-doubt. Instead of focusing on what you are building in your own life, comparison forces you to look outward, causing you to lose track of your personal goals and aspirations. The more you compare, the less content you become with what you already have.*

## FOMO and the Illusion of More

*FOMO often creates a false belief: that there's something "better" out there. That somehow, everyone else is experiencing something more fulfilling, more exciting, or more rewarding than what you're doing at that very moment. But here's the key point—there is no universal "better."*

*What you think you're missing out on may not be what you truly want, nor will it necessarily fulfill you in the way you imagine. In fact, the constant chase for something "better" can leave you feeling more unfulfilled and lost.*

*For example, let's say you see a friend posting about a vacation in an exotic location. You may feel that they are living a more exciting life than yours, and that's a natural response. But what if you don't like traveling? What if that vacation isn't even something you truly desire, but you're pursuing it because of the illusion that it's what you "should" want? The illusion of missing out often confuses us into chasing things that aren't aligned with our true desires.*

## Creating Meaning from Within: The Key to Freedom

The truth is, the only thing you're truly missing out on is the meaning you create in your own life. When you stop comparing your life to others and focus on cultivating your own experiences, you reclaim your power. The fear of missing out loses its grip when you realize that you have the ability to create the life that matters to you. **The beauty of life is not in what you don't have, but in embracing what you do.**

So, the next time you feel that pang of FOMO, pause and ask yourself: What is it about this experience that I feel I'm lacking? Often, the things we feel we're missing aren't as important as we think. Maybe what you really need is not more experiences, but more presence. The ability to savor the moment you're in and appreciate the richness of what you already have.

## The Trap of "The Grass is Always Greener"

The illusion of missing out feeds on the belief that someone else's grass is greener, their life more exciting. It creates a never-ending cycle of wanting what you don't have. But this thinking is dangerous. It's a trap. It keeps you stuck in a constant state of dissatisfaction and yearning for something more. You keep striving for more, only to find that the "more" doesn't bring lasting happiness.

*In reality, the grass is not greener on the other side—it's greener where you water it. If you spend your time tending to your own life, focusing on what's important to you, and nurturing your personal growth, that's where the real fulfillment lies. FOMO fades when you take responsibility for your own happiness and stop giving power to the illusion of missing out.*

## A Final Reflection on the Illusion of Missing Out

*The fear of missing out thrives on the illusion that something better is always out there, just beyond reach. But the truth is that the best moments in life are often the simplest, the ones we overlook while chasing something "better."* **The key to ending FOMO lies not in having more, but in appreciating what you have right now.**

*Instead of focusing on the illusion of more, let's focus on the richness of the present. The beauty of life comes when you choose to fully experience what's in front of you, rather than constantly looking over your shoulder at what others are doing.*

*Remember:* **You're never really missing out. You're simply being called to show up for your own life and make the most of it.**

## 3. The Power of Being Present

### The Beauty of the Present Moment

*In a world filled with distractions and constant stimuli, it's easy to forget the simple yet powerful truth: The present moment is all we truly have. The past is a collection of memories, and the future is uncertain. But the present is where life happens. It's the only moment that is real, and yet, we often overlook it in favor of chasing after future possibilities or comparing ourselves to what others are doing.*

*Being present means fully embracing the current moment—feeling, experiencing, and engaging with what is happening right now, without the pull of distractions or the worry of what you might be missing. The real power of presence lies in its simplicity: It's about allowing yourself to be without the pressure of doing or becoming. This doesn't mean you stop setting goals or planning for the future, but it means you stop sacrificing your peace in the present for the hope of something "better" that may never come.*

### Mindfulness: A Tool for Reclaiming the Moment

*One of the most effective ways to experience the power of being present is through mindfulness—a practice that teaches us to observe our thoughts, feelings, and surroundings without judgment. Mindfulness helps us quiet the noise of FOMO, allowing us to focus on the richness of the present moment instead of worrying about what we might be missing.*

*Mindfulness is not just about meditation—it's about cultivating awareness in every moment. It's about noticing the taste of your food, the warmth of the sun, or the sound of laughter. These small moments, which may seem insignificant, hold the key to greater happiness. When we focus on the present, we stop wishing for something else. We stop looking around and start looking within.*

## The Simple Pleasures of Being Here, Now

*The fear of missing out often comes from a belief that life is better somewhere else, with someone else, or doing something else. But in reality, the magic of life often lies in the simplest moments—the things we overlook in our race to keep up with everyone else. The soft sound of rain against your window, the feeling of your breath as you inhale and exhale, the warmth of a hug from a loved one—these are the moments that give life meaning.*

*When you are present, you create space to truly experience these moments. Rather than feeling a constant desire for something more, you find contentment in the here and now. The true joy in life comes from appreciating what's right in front of you, not in the chase for the next big thing.*

## How Presence Connects You with Others

*One of the most profound effects of being present is the way it deepens your connections with others. How many times have you been in a conversation, only to find your mind wandering, thinking about what you could be doing instead or worrying about something else? Being present means truly listening, engaging, and connecting with others in a way that transcends surface-level interactions.*

*When you give someone your full attention, you create a deeper bond. You allow space for meaningful conversations, and you make people feel seen and heard. This is something that FOMO can steal from us—the ability to truly connect. When you're constantly worried about what you're missing, you're not truly experiencing the person or the moment in front of you.*

## *Practicing Gratitude in the Moment*

*Another powerful aspect of being present is gratitude. When we are mindful, we begin to appreciate what we have instead of longing for what we don't. Gratitude shifts our focus from scarcity to abundance, helping us realize that there is so much in our lives that deserves our attention.*

*Gratitude can be as simple as noticing the beauty around you or taking a moment to acknowledge the people who make a difference in your life. It's about cultivating a sense of appreciation for the present, rather than always seeking the next thing. When we practice gratitude, we stop comparing ourselves to others, and we begin to see how full our lives really are.*

## The Deep Joy of Being Here

*When we are fully present, we can experience a deeper sense of joy. Joy that doesn't depend on external circumstances or future achievements, but joy that comes from within. This joy is not fleeting; it's rooted in the moment. It's a happiness that doesn't require validation, approval, or the perfect conditions—it simply exists because we are here, now.*

*Being present means letting go of the constant need to be somewhere else. It's about surrendering the idea that you must be in a different place, experiencing something "better," or comparing yourself to others. In the end, the most fulfilling moments are the ones where we allow ourselves to be fully engaged with life as it is—without the need for anything to change.*

## *A Final Thought on the Power of Presence*

*In a world that encourages us to chase after more, to be everywhere at once, the power of being present is revolutionary. It's an act of rebellion against the pressure to constantly strive, and it's an invitation to slow down and savor the moment. The more present we are, the more we free ourselves from the grip of FOMO and begin to truly enjoy the life we're living.*

*So, the next time you feel the pull of missing out, remember that what you're really missing is the chance to live the life you have. The present moment is where the magic is. And when you embrace it, you discover that there is no better place to be than right here, right now.*

### *Final Reflection*

*Being present isn't just a skill—it's a mindset. It's the understanding that life is not something to be waited for, but something to be experienced in the moment. In a world that pushes us to look outward, the real treasure lies within. **When you show up for your own life, every moment becomes precious.***

## *4. Letting Go of the Need to Be Everywhere*

## The Allure of Being Everywhere

We live in a world that praises the multitasker, the go-getter, the one who can juggle multiple responsibilities and social events at once. In fact, the idea that we should be everywhere, doing everything, is often seen as a mark of success. But this constant push to be all things to all people is a major contributor to FOMO. We feel this inner drive to show up at every event, join every conversation, and keep our calendars packed, believing that our lives will somehow be more fulfilling if we are constantly in motion.

But here's the truth: You don't have to be everywhere to live a fulfilling life. In fact, the constant need to be everywhere is not only unsustainable, it's counterproductive. The pressure to be involved in everything—whether it's social events, work commitments, or simply keeping up with what's happening in the world—can leave you feeling overwhelmed, exhausted, and disconnected from the things that truly matter.

## The Dangers of Overcommitting

Overcommitting is one of the main consequences of trying to be everywhere. We say yes to things that don't align with our values, priorities, or energy levels, simply because we don't want to miss out or disappoint others. But every "yes" that isn't aligned with your true self is another "no" to your peace, your *time, and your well-being.*

*When we overcommit, we stretch ourselves too thin, and we become burnt out. The more we try to please everyone, the less we are able to focus on the things that genuinely bring us joy and fulfillment. The result? We become less effective, more stressed, and less connected to our own needs.*

## Learning to Say No

*The key to letting go of the need to be everywhere is learning how to say no. Saying no isn't selfish—it's a powerful act of self-care. By saying no to things that don't align with your values or goals, you create space for the things that truly matter. You give yourself the gift of time and energy to focus on what nourishes you.*

*Saying no can feel uncomfortable at first. We live in a culture that often associates saying no with being rude or unhelpful. But in reality, saying no is one of the most important tools for protecting your energy and maintaining your boundaries. When you say no to things that don't serve you, you are saying yes to yourself. You are giving yourself permission to prioritize your peace, your well-being, and your happiness.*

## The Power of Prioritization

*Learning to let go of the need to be everywhere also means learning to prioritize. Not every opportunity, invitation, or demand requires your attention. In fact, not everything is worth your time or energy. By intentionally focusing on what matters most, you free yourself from the chaos of trying to do it all.*

*Start by identifying your core values and goals. What truly matters to you? What aligns with your long-term vision for your life? When you know what's most important, it becomes easier to say no to the things that don't align. Prioritizing the things that nourish you—whether it's your health, your relationships, or your creative pursuits—helps you live more intentionally and with greater peace.*

## The Peace in Simplicity

*Simplifying your life can feel like a radical act in today's fast-paced world, but it is one of the most powerful ways to reclaim your time and energy. When you stop trying to do everything, you can finally appreciate the beauty of simplicity. By clearing away the distractions and unnecessary commitments, you create space for what truly brings you joy.*

*Simplicity allows you to be more present in the moment. You stop worrying about what you might be missing and start appreciating what you have. You no longer feel pulled in a million directions, and you can fully engage in the activities and relationships that matter most to you.*

## The Liberation of Letting Go

*Letting go of the need to be everywhere is a form of liberation. It's about recognizing that your worth is not tied to how busy or popular you are. You don't need to prove anything to anyone. By letting go of the constant pressure to be involved in everything, you give yourself permission to focus on the things that truly fulfill you.*

*This freedom allows you to live more intentionally, without the guilt or fear of missing out. You begin to see that peace comes not from being everywhere, but from being here, in the moment. The more you embrace this mindset, the more you realize that less is often more. Less stress. Less obligation. Less burnout. More joy. More clarity. More self-awareness.*

## Creating Space for What Matters

*The ultimate goal of letting go of the need to be everywhere is to create space for what matters most in your life. When you stop scattering your energy across a million different things, you make room for deeper connections, more meaningful experiences, and greater fulfillment. You allow yourself to dive into the things that bring you peace, joy, and purpose.*

*It's in this space that you begin to live authentically. You stop living for the approval of others and start living for yourself. You stop measuring your worth by how many events you attend or how many people you know, and start measuring it by the depth of your relationships, the clarity of your intentions, and the fulfillment you find in your life.*

## Final Thoughts on Letting Go

*Letting go of the need to be everywhere is one of the most profound steps you can take in your journey toward inner peace. It's about releasing the societal pressure to constantly perform, constantly strive, and constantly be "on." Instead, it's about choosing to slow down, simplify, and savor the moments that matter most.*

*So, let go. Let go of the need to be everywhere. Let go of the constant drive to do it all. Embrace the power of presence, the beauty of simplicity, and the peace that comes with creating a life that is truly your own.*

## Reflection

*Remember, **you don't need to be everywhere to be at peace.** By letting go of the pressure to constantly be "on," you free yourself to experience the beauty of life as it unfolds, one moment at a time.*

## 5. Reclaiming Your Time and Energy

### The Cost of Wasting Time

*In today's fast-paced world, time often feels like the one thing we never have enough of. Between work, social obligations, and the constant barrage of notifications and distractions, it's easy to feel like we're always running on empty. We give our time away to things that don't truly nourish us—whether it's scrolling endlessly through social media, attending events that don't serve us, or trying to meet everyone else's expectations.*

*But here's a truth we often forget: Time is our most precious resource. Once it's gone, we can never get it back. Yet, we often spend it on things that don't bring us any real fulfillment. The power of reclaiming your time is about recognizing that you don't have to give it away to everything that demands it. Instead, you have the power to choose how to spend it and on what truly matters.*

### The Power of Boundaries

*The first step in reclaiming your time and energy is setting boundaries. Boundaries are essential for protecting your mental and emotional well-being. Without them, you risk burning out, losing focus, and losing yourself in the demands of others.*

*Boundaries come in many forms: physical, emotional, and time-related. They are about saying "no" when necessary, without feeling guilty, and about saying "yes" only when it truly aligns with your values. Boundaries help you take control of your time by defining what is acceptable and what is not.*

*Setting boundaries is not about being rigid or unkind; it's about being clear about your priorities. When you create healthy boundaries, you allow yourself to focus on what matters most, whether it's your personal growth, relationships, or creative pursuits. Boundaries protect your energy, so you can spend it on things that are truly fulfilling.*

## The Art of Prioritization

*Once you've set boundaries, it's time to start prioritizing. Prioritization is the process of determining what's most important and making it a focal point in your life. It's about deciding where to direct your time and energy, so that you're not spreading yourself too thin on things that don't contribute to your well-being or long-term goals.*

*The challenge here is to identify what truly brings you joy and fulfillment. Often, we are pulled in different directions by external pressures, but prioritizing means making space for what aligns with your authentic self. This might mean cutting back on social obligations, spending less time on distractions, or saying no to opportunities that don't align with your personal goals.*

*It's helpful to start by identifying your core values and what you want your life to represent. Is your time best spent advancing your career? Is it about nurturing relationships with loved ones? Or is it about dedicating time to your personal passions and growth? Once you have clarity on what matters most, it becomes easier to prioritize your actions, allowing you to reclaim your time and energy from the pull of FOMO.*

**Learning to Enjoy Solitude**

*Another essential aspect of reclaiming your time is learning to enjoy solitude. In a world where we are constantly surrounded by noise, people, and distractions, solitude is often seen as something to avoid. However, solitude offers a unique opportunity for self-reflection, creativity, and personal growth. It's in these quiet moments that we are able to reconnect with ourselves and our true desires.*

*Spending time alone is not the same as being lonely—it's a chance to recharge, reflect, and focus on your inner world. In solitude, you have the space to reconnect with your values, clarify your goals, and discover what truly brings you fulfillment.*

*Solitude allows you to break free from the noise of others and listen to your own inner voice. By making time for solitude, you create the mental and emotional space necessary to truly understand what matters most in your life, helping you reclaim your time and energy in a meaningful way.*

### Disconnecting from Distractions

*The digital age has given us an abundance of distractions. Social media, emails, news updates, and constant notifications keep us constantly on edge, feeling like we need to be aware of everything all the time. But in reality, these distractions only pull us further away from living in the moment and reclaiming our time.*

*The key to overcoming these distractions is learning how to disconnect. This doesn't mean completely abandoning technology or social media, but rather setting intentional boundaries for when and how you engage with it. Consider scheduling tech-free time each day, turning off notifications, or setting specific times for checking social media and emails. This gives you more control over your time, preventing endless scrolling or checking your phone from taking over your life.*

*Disconnecting from distractions also means choosing to engage with things that truly nourish you—whether that's reading a book, spending time with loved ones, pursuing a creative project, or simply resting. By disconnecting from distractions, you free up time and energy for the things that matter most.*

### Reclaiming Your Energy

*It's not just about time—it's about energy. Reclaiming your energy is just as important as reclaiming your time. Every task, commitment, and interaction you have requires energy, and if you're not careful, you can quickly deplete yourself without even realizing it. That's why it's important to choose where to invest your energy wisely.*

*Energy comes from taking care of yourself—mentally, emotionally, and physically. Prioritize activities that rejuvenate you, such as exercising, eating well, meditating, or simply resting. When you take care of your body and mind, you ensure that you have the energy to focus on the things that are truly meaningful to you.*

*Reclaiming your energy also involves learning to let go of things that drain you—whether it's toxic relationships, negative self-talk, or unproductive habits. As you clear away the sources of energy depletion, you create space for the activities and people that fill you with vitality and purpose.*

### The Gift of Time Well Spent

*Reclaiming your time and energy is ultimately about living a life of intention. It's about choosing to invest in the things that matter most to you, not out of obligation or fear of missing out, but because they bring you joy, fulfillment, and growth.*

*When you make conscious choices about where to spend your time and energy, you begin to feel more at peace. You stop being reactive to external demands and start living proactively. You take control of your life, rather than letting life control you.*

*By reclaiming your time and energy, you stop allowing distractions and obligations to dictate your happiness. Instead, you create a life that aligns with your values, your desires, and your true purpose. You learn to savor each moment, live in the present, and invest in the things that bring you lasting fulfillment.*

## *Final Reflection*

*When you reclaim your time and energy, you are giving yourself the gift of a life well lived—one where you are not constantly pulled in every direction by the pressure of FOMO, but instead are present, intentional, and fully engaged with the things that truly matter. You choose to live in a way that nourishes your soul and brings you the peace and fulfillment that come from living on your own terms.*

*Reclaiming your time and energy is not just about making better choices—it's about choosing yourself. In a world full of distractions and demands, it's easy to lose track of what truly matters. But when you begin to live intentionally, to focus on what fuels your soul, you create a life that is uniquely yours. You free yourself from the chains of FOMO and reconnect with the present, where the real beauty of life unfolds.*

*As you start saying no to the noise and yes to what nourishes you, you find peace in the simplicity of now. You create space for joy, for growth, for quiet moments, and for deeper connections. Every decision you make about your time becomes an act of self-love—a reminder that you are worthy of the life you desire.*

*Remember, the essence of life is not in the quantity of moments, but in the quality of how you spend them. By reclaiming your time, you embrace the freedom to live a life that is true to you. And in that truth, you find a peace that FOMO can never take away.*

*The present moment is all you truly have. In it, lies all the richness of life, the simplicity of joy, and the depth of connection. Let go of the need to chase; instead, embrace what you already have.*

## CHAPTER FOURTEEN

# THE TRUTH IS, LIFE WILL NEVER BE PERFECT.

*From the very beginning, we are taught to chase perfection—whether it's in our achievements, appearances, or relationships. Society tells us that a perfect life is the one without flaws, without failures, without any room for mistakes. But in reality, life is messy. It's unpredictable, filled with both triumphs and struggles. We'll face setbacks that challenge us, mistakes that humble us, and moments that leave us questioning our decisions. But here's the secret: **those imperfections**—those challenges and mistakes—are not roadblocks; they are the things that give life its richness, depth, and meaning.*

***We will make mistakes. We will face setbacks. We will encounter challenges.** And while it might feel overwhelming or discouraging at times, it's these very things that define our journey. Every misstep, every* challenge, is an opportunity to grow and evolve. The idea that life should be flawless is a myth that causes unnecessary pressure, guilt, and dissatisfaction. **In truth, it's the imperfections that make the journey worthwhile.** It's the contrast between struggle and success, darkness and light, failure and triumph, that creates the beautiful narrative of our lives.

The key to living a life without regret, then, isn't about trying to avoid mistakes or sidestepping challenges. It's about **owning** them. It's about acknowledging when we stumble, learning from those stumbles, and not allowing them to define us. When we can embrace our mistakes—not as failures but as lessons—**we create space for growth**. The truth is, it's the mistakes we make and the failures we encounter that teach us who we really are and what we're truly capable of.

It's not about avoiding hardship—it's about rising after each fall, having the courage to pick ourselves back up. **The courage to move forward** despite the weight of past mistakes, despite the fear of judgment, and despite the voices around us that tell us to quit. It's about **being resilient**, about showing up for yourself, even when the world doesn't seem to have your back. Each time you fall and rise again, you strengthen not only your resolve but also your understanding of yourself.

**The pursuit of perfection**—of living a life that is free from error or imperfection—is a constant battle. We *are often told that if we're not perfect, we're failing. But it's in this pursuit of perfection that we often miss the beauty of living authentically. We get lost in comparing ourselves to others, in trying to measure up to unrealistic standards, in trying to be who we're not. But **the weight of perfection** is a burden that no one can truly carry. It's exhausting, and it robs us of the joy that comes with just being human.*

*We also live in a world that loves to judge. We're afraid to step out of line, to make mistakes, because of what others will think of us. **The fear of judgment** can paralyze us and prevent us from pursuing our dreams, speaking our truths, or even making small decisions that could lead to greater happiness. The fear of being criticized, of being misunderstood, of being "less than" someone else—it's real. But if we let this fear dictate our lives, we will never truly live. Instead, we'll spend our days conforming to what we think others expect of us, never daring to be who we really are.*

*And then, there's the weight of **other people's expectations**. Whether it's family, friends, or society as a whole, we often feel pressured to live according to someone else's version of success. We chase degrees, promotions, relationships, or status to meet expectations that may not even align with who we are. But in the end, it's our own vision of success that matters. No one else's opinion can define your journey or your happiness.*

*Yet, through all of this—the mistakes, the setbacks, the judgments, and the pressures—we still have one thing that no one can take away: **the ability to rise again**. It's the resilience to stand up after we've been knocked down. It's the courage to keep moving forward, even when the road ahead looks uncertain. It's about saying, "I may have failed, but that doesn't define me." It's about learning, growing, and choosing to keep going, no matter how many times we stumble along the way.*

*When we embrace this, when we stop fearing failure and judgment, we can look back on our lives with a deep sense of fulfillment. We'll be able to say, "I lived fully." Not because our lives were free of mistakes, but because we were brave enough to take risks, to learn from our challenges, and to continuously evolve. When you live authentically—when you accept that mistakes are part of your story, and that setbacks are just stepping stones—**you will discover a deeper peace** that comes not from perfection, but from embracing everything that makes you who you are.*

*And in the end, isn't that what we all want? To live fully, without regret? To look back on our journey and say, "Yes, I gave it my all. I embraced the messy, imperfect, beautiful ride of life. And I wouldn't change a thing."*

..

### The Courage to Let Go

*One of the most profound—and most difficult—lessons life will ever teach you is this:* **sometimes, the greatest act of strength is the act of letting go.**

*We often cling tightly to the things that feel familiar, even when they hurt us. We hold on to toxic relationships, not because they make us happy, but because the idea of loneliness terrifies us more. We stay stuck in draining jobs, not because they fulfill our souls, but because the unknown future feels riskier than the misery we already know. We chase dreams that no longer ignite our hearts, simply because we once said we would. And in doing so, we carry heavy burdens that were never meant to be carried for so long.*

*Letting go is not a sign of weakness.* **It is an act of reclaiming your life.**

*It is not the loss of a part of you—it's the recovery of who you are underneath the weight of everything you were never meant to hold. It takes tremendous courage to say, "This no longer serves me, and I choose to release it." It takes strength to walk away from what you once thought you couldn't live without, only to discover you are so much stronger without it.*

*We are often taught that loyalty means staying. That perseverance means never giving up. That strength is in enduring whatever life throws at you without ever stepping away. But the truth is—sometimes* **true loyalty is to your own soul,** *and sometimes perseverance means having the bravery to say, "This is not my path anymore."*

*The pursuit of perfection also chains us down. It makes us believe that unless everything goes exactly as planned, we are failures. That if we stumble, we have somehow lost our worth. We become so obsessed with perfect timelines, flawless outcomes, and unbroken records, that we miss the raw, vibrant beauty of the imperfect life unfolding in front of us.*

**Letting go of perfection is letting go of the lie that you have to be flawless to be worthy.**
*It's understanding that your value was never tied to how perfectly you perform, but to how honestly you live.*

*And detachment? It's not about becoming cold, distant, or emotionless. It's about no longer allowing your happiness to be dictated by things outside of your control. It's about releasing the exhausting need to control how others see you, how your plans unfold, or how every chapter of your story is written.*

**Detachment is freeing.**
*It's the soul whispering, "I trust myself enough to flow*

*with life, not against it."*

*It's learning to walk away when the door refuses to open. It's choosing peace over chaos, growth over comfort, and freedom over fear.*

*Letting go means allowing yourself to grieve—because yes, there will be grief. It means honoring the part of you that tried so hard, loved so deeply, and hoped so earnestly. But it also means recognizing that you deserve more than just surviving—you deserve to* **thrive.**

*You deserve relationships that nourish you, work that ignites you, dreams that still set your soul on fire.*
*And when something no longer does that, you owe it to yourself to release it—not out of bitterness, but out of love for the life that is still waiting for you.*

*The person you thought you needed to be?*
*The dreams you thought you had to chase?*
*The approval you believed you had to earn?*
*You can let them go.*

*Because* **you are enough**—*even without the things you thought once defined you.*

*In the end, letting go is not about giving up. It's about* **giving yourself back** *to yourself.*

## *Embracing Your Journey*

*Living a life without regret doesn't mean you will never question yourself.*
*It doesn't mean you won't sometimes lie awake at night, wondering if a different choice might have led you somewhere else, to someone else, to something seemingly "better."*
*It doesn't mean you'll never wonder what could have been.*
*It means understanding this:* **every decision you made, every path you walked, even the detours and the mistakes, built the person you are today.**
*And that person—you, right now—is already worthy.*
*Already enough. Already a story worth telling.*

*We often grow up believing that the "right" path will be obvious. That life will hand us a perfectly drawn map, with all the right turns marked clearly. But reality is far messier than that.*
**Life isn't a straight line—it's a maze, a spiral, a dance between certainty and chaos.**

*You will lose your way.*
*You will question your steps.*
*You will have seasons where the fog is so thick that you can barely see your own hands in front of you.*
*But here's the truth:* **not knowing exactly where**

**you're going is where real life begins.**


*It's in the uncertainty that magic happens.*
*It's when you don't have all the answers that you're most open to the breathtaking surprises life has waiting for you.*
*The best parts of your story will not be the parts you planned—but the parts you discovered when you dared to trust the journey.*


*Life isn't about "getting it right" all the time.*
*It's not about arriving at some perfect destination where everything finally makes sense.*
***It's about living it—fully, imperfectly, boldly.***


*When you embrace your journey, you stop measuring your timeline against someone else's highlight reel.*
*You stop punishing yourself for not having it all figured out by a certain age.*
*You stop waiting for the perfect moment, the perfect version of yourself, the perfect set of circumstances.*


*Instead, you start living **now**.*
*You start seeing beauty in the broken roads, strength in the scars, wisdom in the wounds.*
*You realize that the messiness, the uncertainty, the wrong turns—they weren't detours.*
*They were the journey.*

*You are not late.*
*You are not lost.*
*You are not behind.*
**You are exactly where you are meant to be, learning**
**exactly what you are meant to learn.**


*When you choose to embrace your life as it is—with*
*all its imperfections—you unlock a level of peace that*
*perfection could never offer.*
*You stop seeking validation from the outside world*
*and start finding fulfillment within yourself.*


*Because in the end, it was never about racing to some*
*perfect ending.*
*It was always about learning to dance through the*
*storms, to laugh through the failures, to love even*
*when it hurts, and to keep moving forward with hope*
*stitched into every step.*


**Your journey is yours alone.**
**Own it.**
**Love it.**
**And live it with everything you've got.**


**The Freedom in Saying Yes to Yourself**

*As you move through life's endless crossroads, remember this simple but powerful truth:*
**Every choice you make is either a step toward yourself or a step away from yourself.**

*Saying "yes" to yourself is one of the bravest things you will ever do.*
*It's not just a choice—it's a revolution.*
*It's reclaiming your voice in a world that keeps trying to silence it.*
*It's refusing to shrink just to fit into someone else's comfort zone.*
*It's standing tall in your truth, even when your hands are shaking.*

*When you say "yes" to yourself, you're not being selfish—you're being alive.*
*You are choosing to prioritize your own happiness, your own peace, your own dreams.*
*You are recognizing that your well-being matters, not because someone else says it does, but because **you** know it does.*

*The most beautiful part?*
**You don't need anyone's permission to live your truth.**
*You don't need a stamp of approval, a round of applause, or a nod from the world.*
*The quiet conviction in your heart is enough.*

*Saying "yes" to yourself is an act of rebellion against everything that told you to settle, to stay silent, to live small.*
*It's about choosing a life that feels good on the inside, not just one that looks good on the outside.*

*But here's the other side of it—saying "yes" to yourself also means you must learn the courage to say "no" without guilt.*

*"No" to the people who drain your energy.*
*"No" to the paths that don't light your soul on fire.*
*"No" to the versions of yourself that you have outgrown.*
***No*** *to anything that demands you betray yourself in the process of pleasing others.*

*Saying "no" is not cruelty. It's clarity.*
*It's the realization that your time, your energy, your dreams—they are sacred ground.*
*Not everyone gets access to them. Not everything deserves your attention.*

*Every "no" you speak is a wall built to protect the garden you are growing within.*
*And every "yes" you whisper to yourself is a seed planted in that garden—a promise that you are choosing **you**.*

*Imagine waking up every morning knowing that you're not just surviving—you're thriving.*
*Not because life is perfect, but because you are finally living it on your own terms.*
*You are breathing in your own air, dreaming your own dreams, writing your own story.*

*When you say "yes" to yourself, the regret of living someone else's life begins to dissolve like mist in the morning sun.*
*In its place, something powerful blooms—**freedom**.*

*Freedom to be exactly who you are.*
*Freedom to chase what sets your heart on fire.*
*Freedom to live so fully, so fiercely, that even the scars you gather along the way shine like medals of honor.*

*You are the author.*
*You are the architect.*
*You are the masterpiece.*

**Say yes. And watch yourself become everything you were always meant to be.**

### Living a Life True to You

*At the end of it all, when the noise fades and the world's expectations fall silent, the life you have lived will be yours and yours alone.*

*Not your parents' life.*
*Not society's version.*
*Not your friends' or critics' imagined paths for you.*
**Just yours.**


*You weren't born to live for applause, approval, or fleeting validation.*
*You were born to live a life that feels right in your soul, even if it looks different from everyone else's.*
*You were born to chase dreams that may not make sense to anyone but you.*
*You were born to set your own standards—to carve your own way, even if no one understands it.*


*The people you meet, the heartbreaks you endure, the mountains you climb, the failures that crack you open—all of it, every beautiful and brutal piece, shapes the person you are becoming.*
*Not perfect.*
*Not flawless.*
**But real. Alive. Honest. Free.**


*The moment you stop measuring yourself against the lives around you, you unlock something precious: your freedom.*
*You realize that your worth was never tied to how many people liked you, applauded you, or approved of you.*
*Your worth has always lived inside you—unshaken, untouchable.*

*Living true to yourself means daring to follow your own compass, even when the path is uncertain.*
*It means choosing authenticity over approval.*
*It means believing that your dreams, your voice, and your heart matter—not because someone else says they do, but because you know they do.*


*And when you begin to live this way—raw, real, fully—you discover a new kind of power.*
**The power to live without regret.**


*Because the truth is, regrets are not born from the things you dared to do.*
*Regrets are born from the dreams you abandoned.*
*The words you swallowed.*
*The love you didn't fight for.*
*The risks you were too scared to take.*


*It's not the failures that will haunt you.*
*It's the chances you were too afraid to grab with both hands.*


*But here's the most beautiful truth:*
**You still have time.**
*As long as you are breathing, you have time to chase what sets your soul ablaze.*
*To speak your truth.*
*To love without fear.*
*To live so boldly that even your scars will tell a story of courage.*

*You are not here to live someone else's life.*
*You are here to live yours.*
*Unapologetically.*
*Unashamedly.*
*Unstoppably.*


*So choose you.*
*Choose the dream.*
*Choose the unknown.*
*Choose the life that leaves you breathless with wonder.*
*Choose the path where you can look back, no matter how messy it gets, and whisper to yourself:*


**"I lived. Truly, deeply, and without regret."**

***Final Thought:***

*"Regret is not found in the choices you make, but in the fear that kept you from making them. Live*

*with courage, live with authenticity, and live without looking back."*

248

*with courage, live with authenticity, and live without looking back."*

## CHAPTER FIFTEEN

# THE ART OF DISAPPEARING

*Disappearing doesn't mean you stop existing.*
*It means you stop needing to exist for others.*


*You become silent.*
*You stop explaining yourself.*
*You stop reaching out first.*
*You stop expecting anyone to understand.*


*You pull back — slowly, carefully — until you are just*
*a ghost to the world.*


*It hurts at first.*
*You'll want someone to notice.*
*You'll hope someone will come searching for you.*


*But no one does.*
*And that's when you realize: maybe it was never about*

*you.*
*Maybe it was always just about what you could give them.*

*The art of disappearing is not about hating people.*
*It's about choosing yourself, even when it feels lonely.*
*It's about understanding that sometimes you have to walk away, not because you don't care —*
*but because staying is destroying you.*

*You stop answering calls you don't want to answer.*
*You stop attending events where you feel invisible.*
*You stop pretending to be fine when you're breaking inside.*

*You disappear from the places you don't belong anymore.*

*You become quieter, calmer.*
*You watch more.*
*You speak less.*
*You exist in the background —*
*and somehow, it becomes enough.*

*One day, you realize you don't miss the noise.*
*You don't miss the pretending.*
*You don't miss the people who never really saw you in the first place.*

*And you finally understand:*
**You were never meant to be for everyone.**


Why Do People Disappear?


*Sometimes, people don't disappear because they hate life.*
*They disappear because life doesn't feel real to them anymore.*


*They get tired of acting like everything is okay.*
*They get tired of carrying a weight that nobody else can see.*


*The smile becomes fake.*
*The conversations become empty.*
*And every day feels like putting on a mask that's way too heavy.*


*Disappearing feels like the only honest thing left.*


*It's not because they gave up.*
*It's because the fight inside them got too loud, and they just wanted peace —*
*even if that peace meant becoming invisible.*

*"You... have broken your pact with the mountain. Therefore the mountain... can no longer take any responsibility for your life", "It's not just about climbing, it's about the struggle, isolation, and pushing yourself beyond what you think you're capable of", and "We need to have a mask that we never take off"*

*-The climber*

*A Small Story I Never Told*

*There was a time — not that long ago — when I would walk in the middle of the night.*
*No music. No phone. No destination.*

*Just me and the darkness.*

*It wasn't about running away.*
*It was about trying to find a place where my heart didn't feel so heavy.*
*Sometimes, the cold air was the only thing that made me feel alive.*

*Sometimes, I would look up at the stars and think,*
***"Maybe somewhere up there, there's a version of me that's not broken."***

*But the stars never answered.*
*They just kept shining, silently.*


*And maybe that's what life is too —*
*silent, distant, beautiful, but not always here to save*
*you.*


*"Preoccupied with a single leaf... you won't see the*
*tree"*


*-vegabond*


*The Price of Disappearing*


*But listen...*


*Disappearing is not a dream.*
*It's not something you should chase.*


*It's painful.*
*It's empty.*
*It leaves you cold, even when the sun is shining.*

*I'm not writing this to inspire you.*
*I'm writing this to warn you.*


*Don't end up like me.*
*Don't let the world turn you into a ghost.*


*Keep your light.*
*Keep your love.*
*Even when it hurts —*
**Stay.**


*Because disappearing might feel peaceful...*
*but in the end, it's just another way of dying while*
*you're still breathing.*


*"Disappearing isn't an escape. It's just another form*
*of dying without ever truly living."*


*"I haven't told you what I truly want or what I'm going*
*to do because sometimes, not saying anything is its*
*own kind of answer — silence speaks louder than any*
*words could."*

And so, we reach the end.
But this isn't a conclusion.
It's a beginning.
The art of not caring is not something you master once and for all—it's a practice.
A choice you make every day, sometimes every hour.
It's the freedom to walk away from what doesn't serve you,
and the strength to stay present with what does.
Maybe you're still on your journey,
still learning how to let go of the weight you've carried for so long.
Maybe you'll never fully stop caring.
But what matters is this:
You now have the power to choose where your care goes,
and what's worth your energy.
If you're tired, it's okay to rest.
If you're unsure, it's okay to pause.
But never forget this—
you are not the sum of other people's expectations.
You are not the mistakes you've made.
You are not the roles you've been forced to play.
You are enough as you are.
You always have been.
So walk into the world with your heart in your hands,
untouched by the noise.
Free to feel what you want to feel,
and free to let go of what you don't.
This is your art.
The art of not caring.
or
The Philosophy of Not Giving a Damn
— [the stellar nomad]